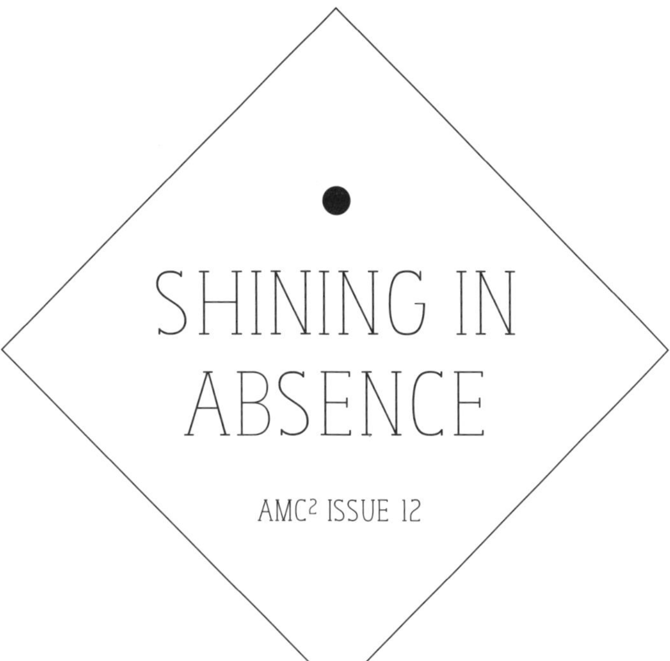

DEDICATED TO
FRIDO TROOST 1960-2013

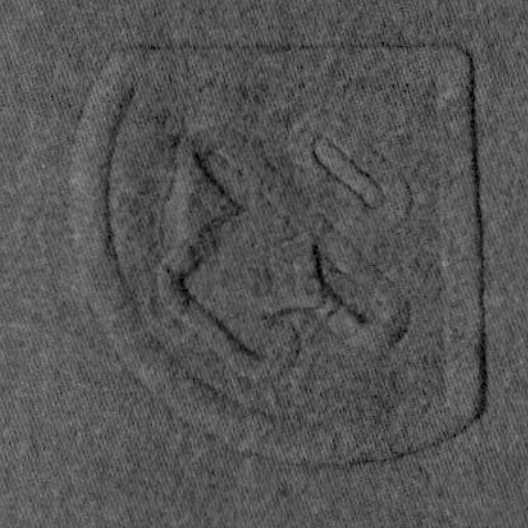

Sport im

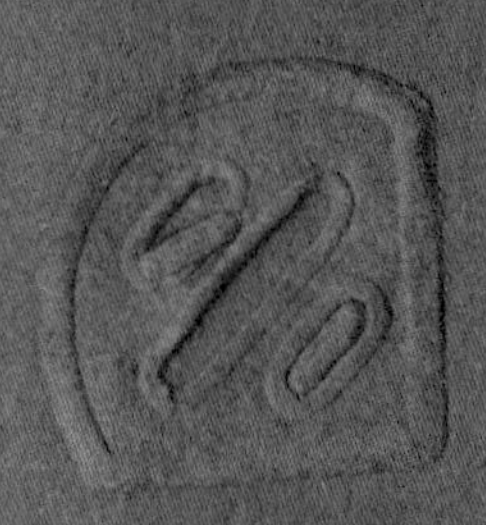

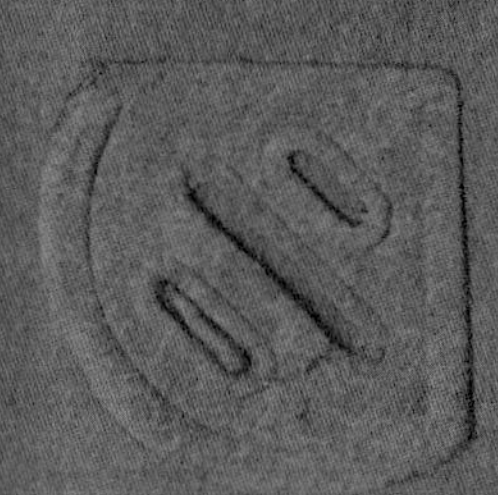

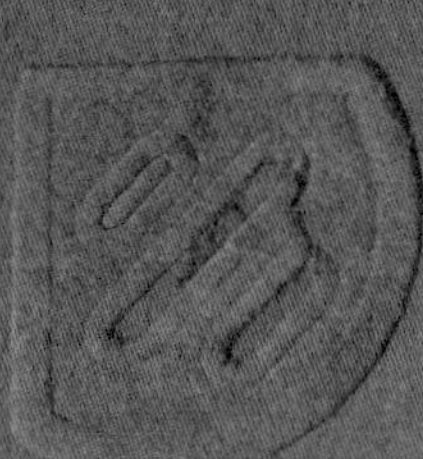

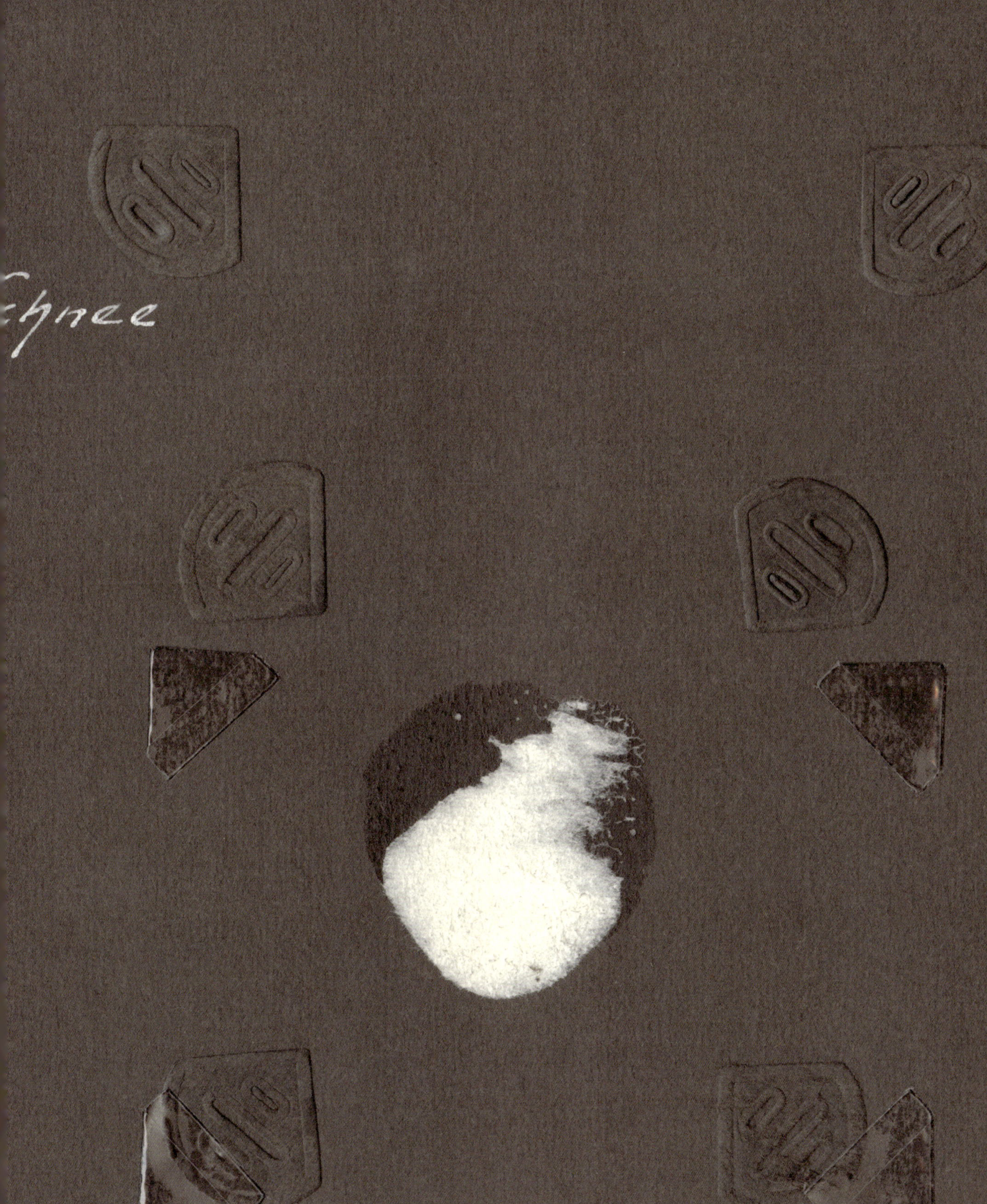

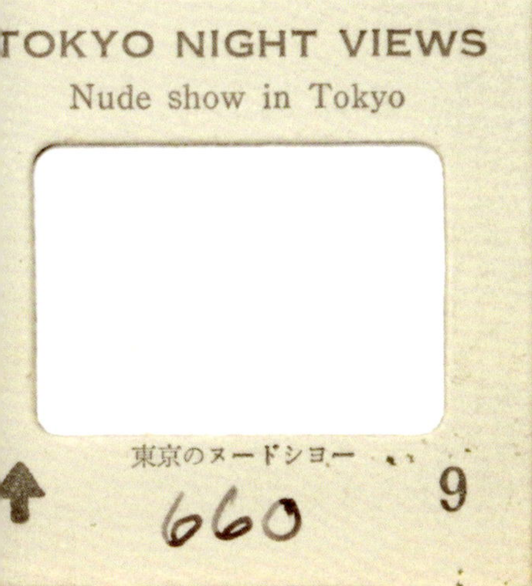
TOKYO NIGHT VIEWS
Nude show in Tokyo
東京のヌードショー
9
660

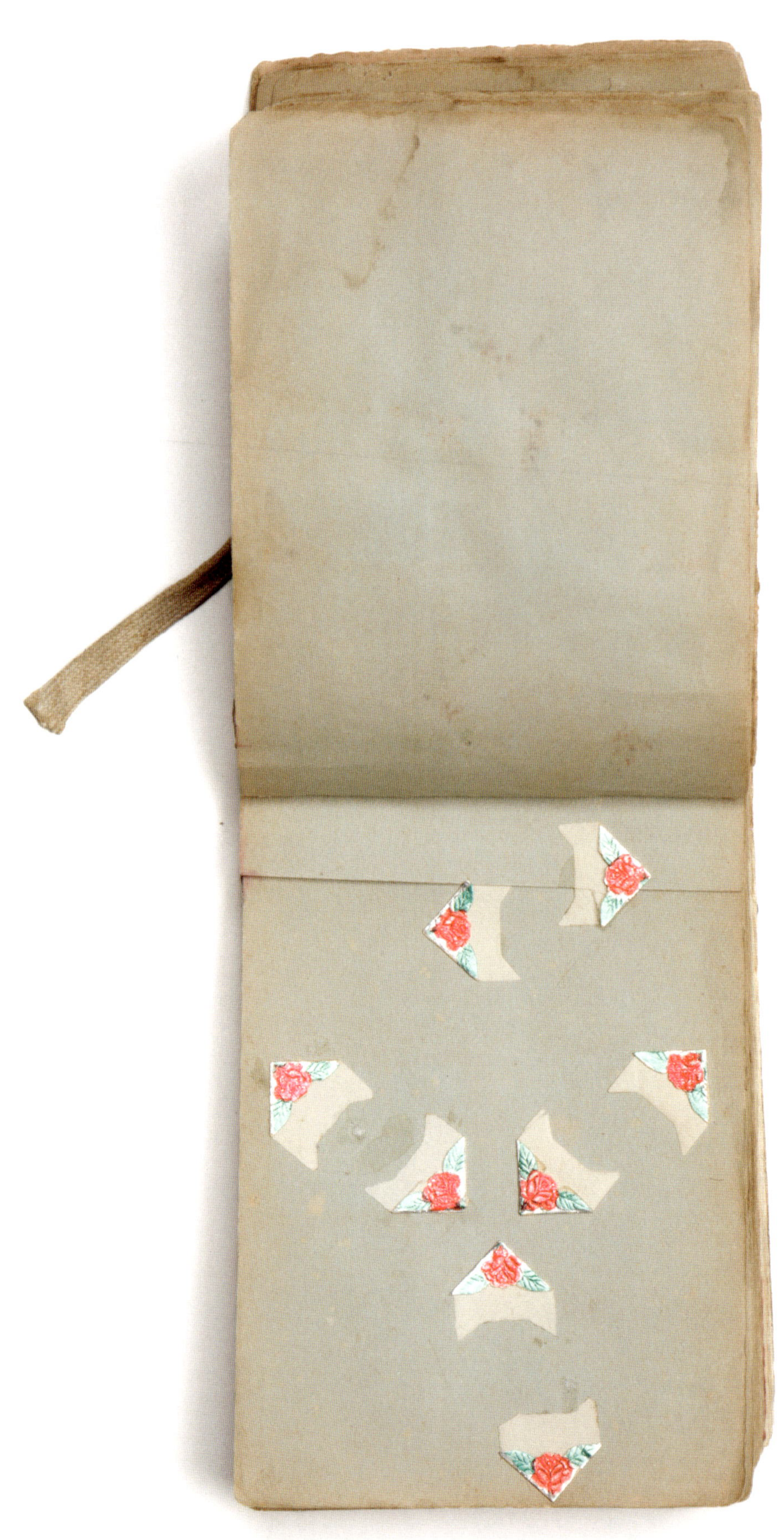

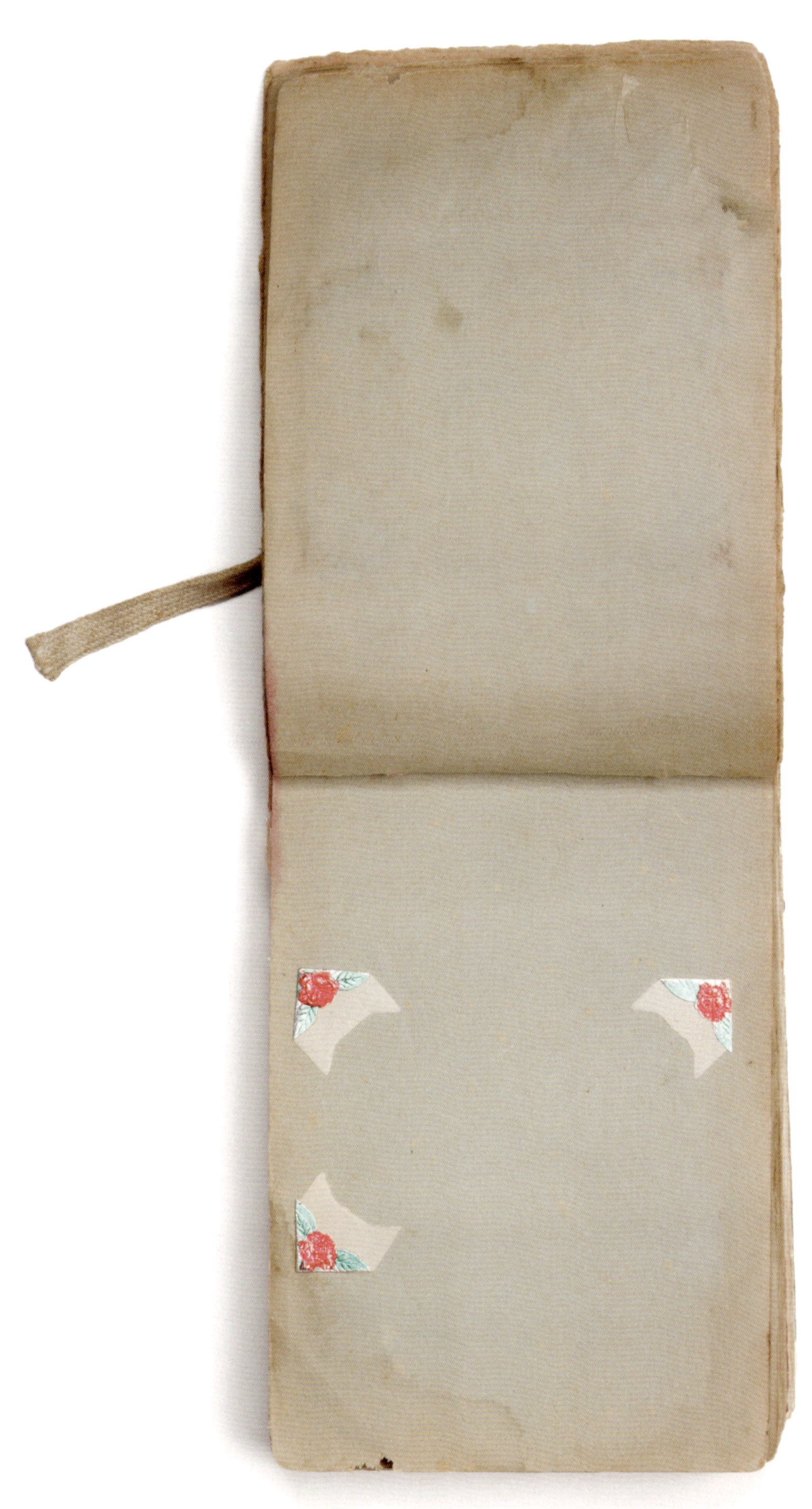

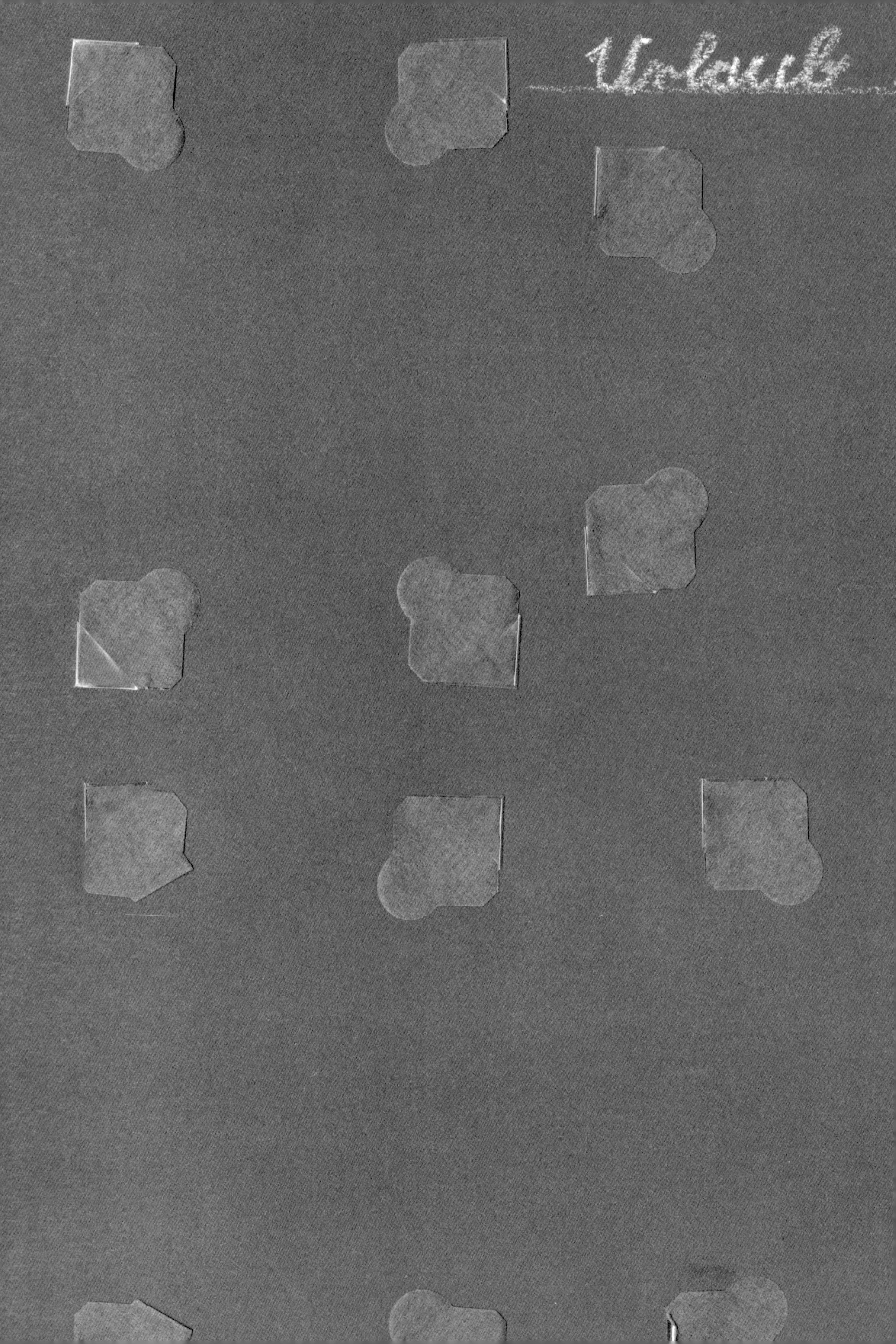
Urlaub

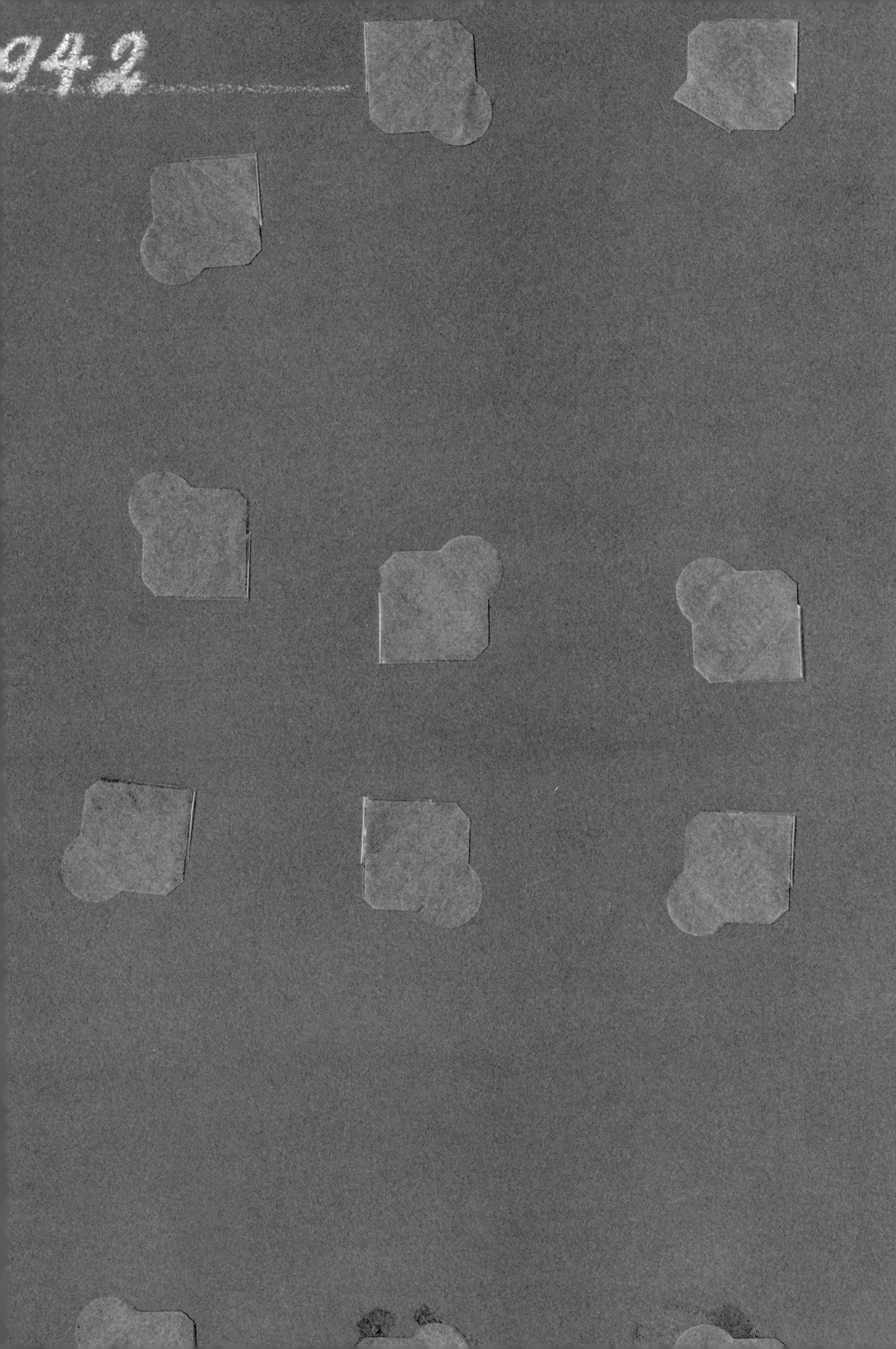
942

Marie og Niels Kornbo[?]

Preb[...]

Familie billedet fra Aarhus

ndeme

Helene Haldsmand

Læge Falskid Jensen Vammen

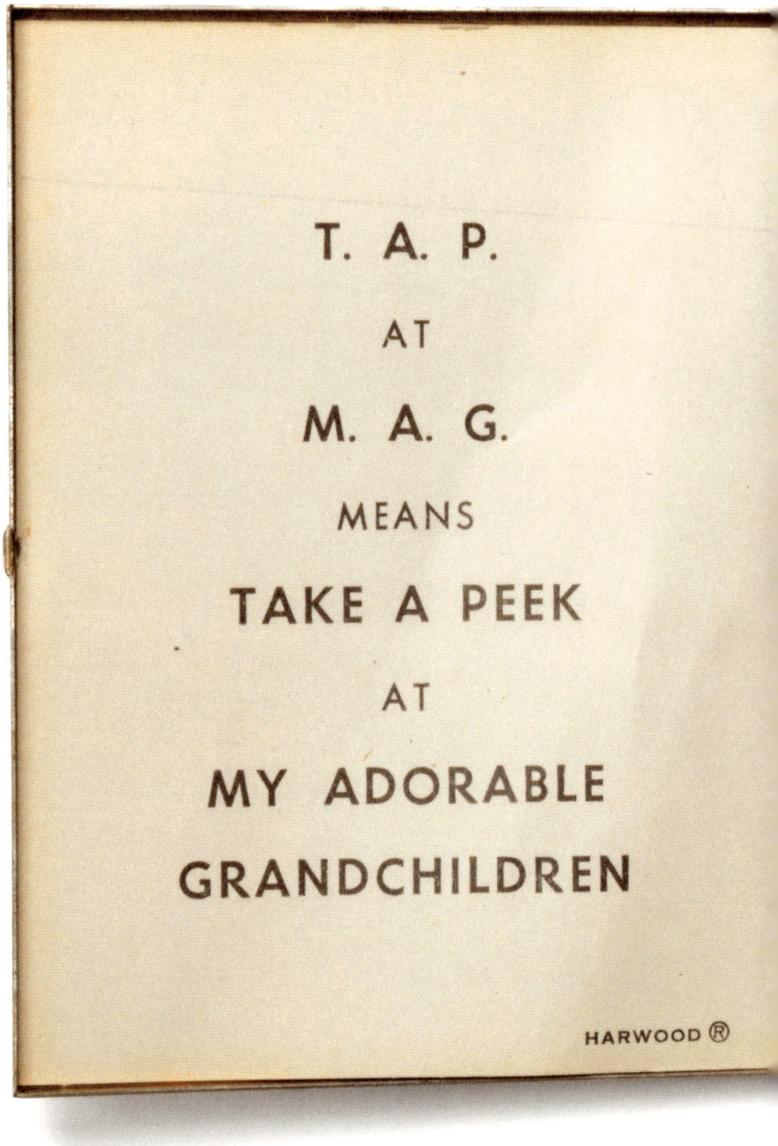

T. A. P.

AT

M. A. G.

MEANS

TAKE A PEEK

AT

MY ADORABLE

GRANDCHILDREN

HARWOOD ®

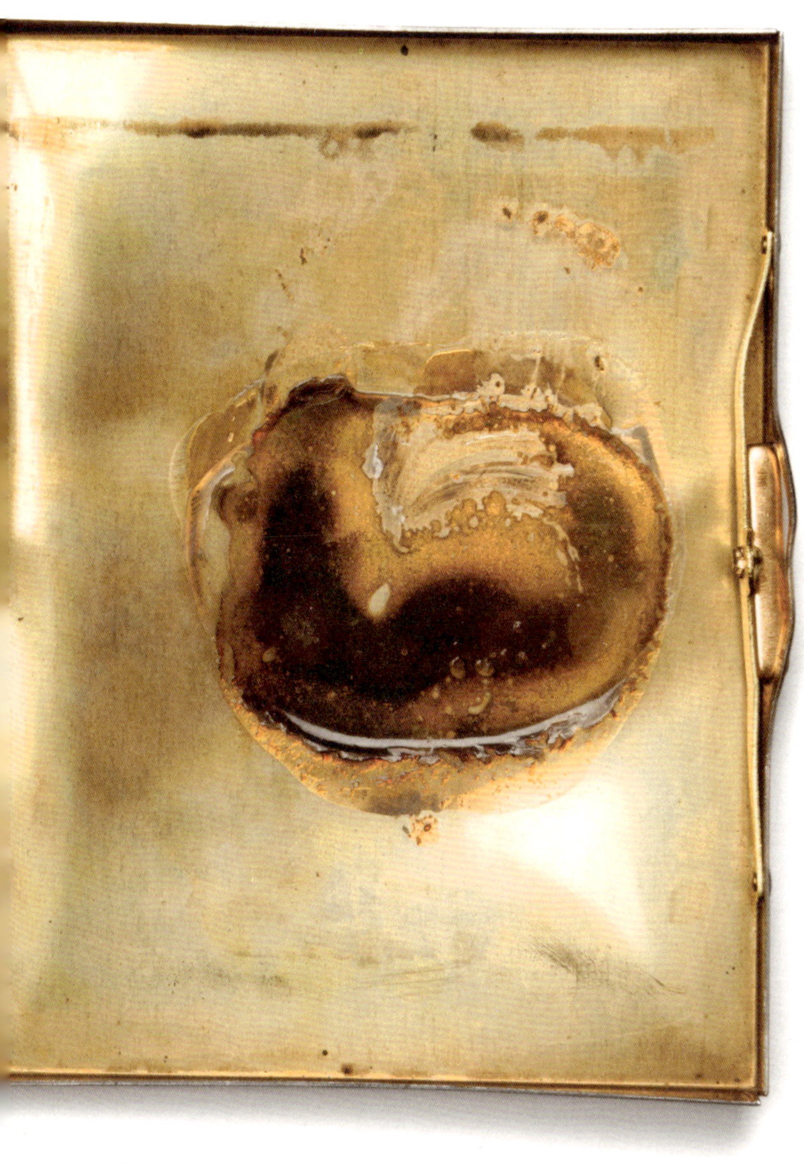

od 13. do 15.

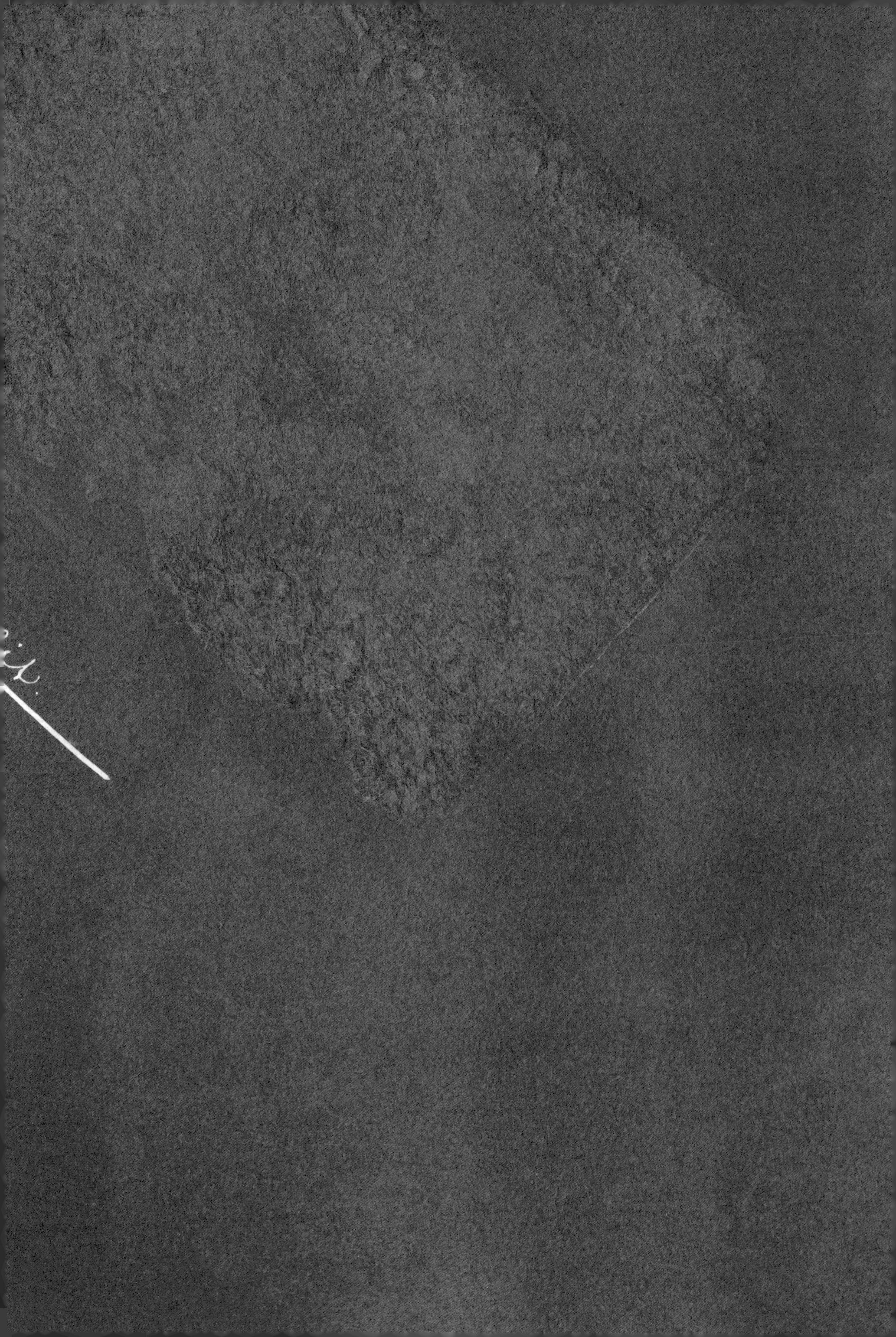

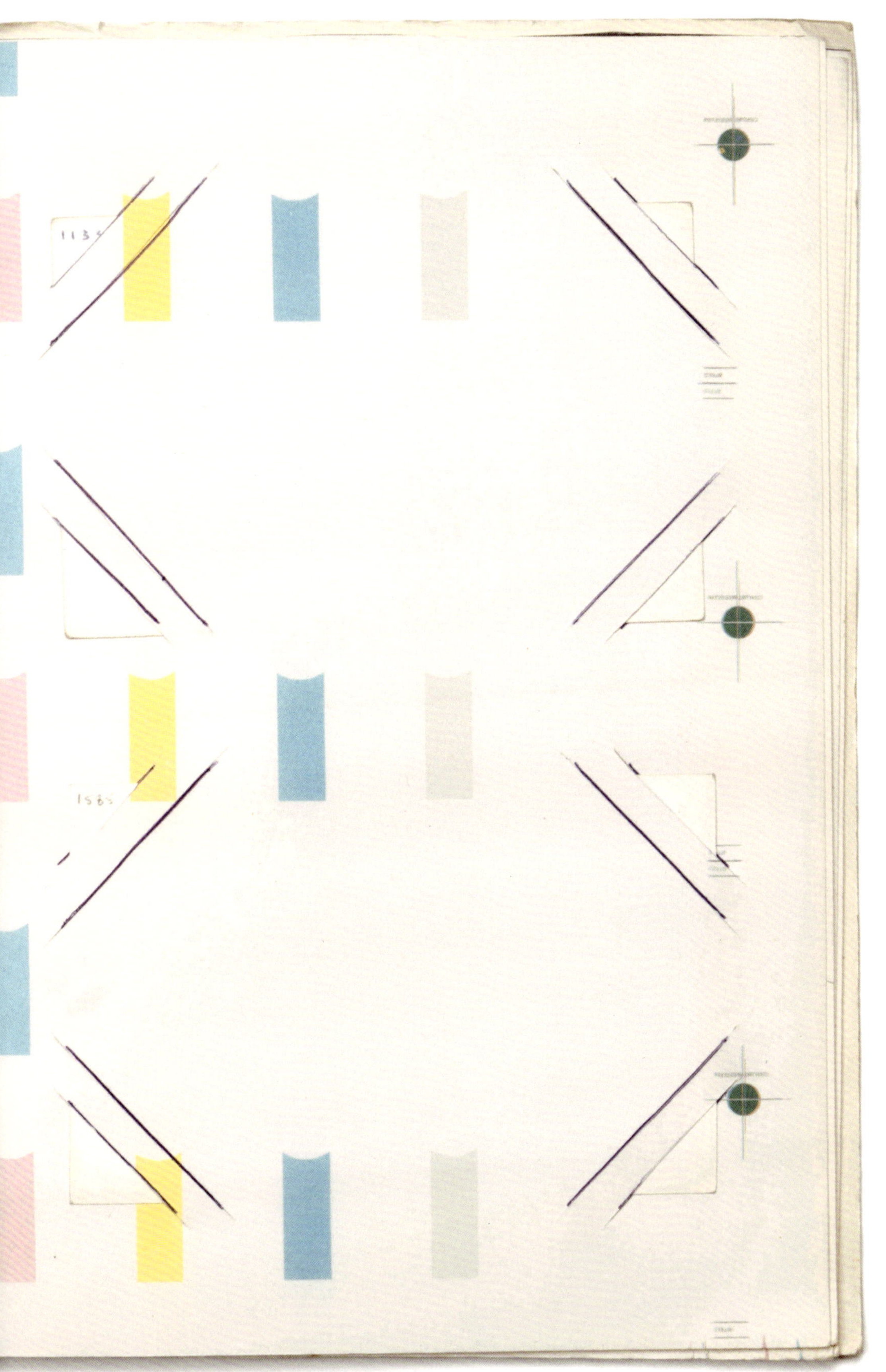

1982. 4. 26

指水上品公

五車门

BEAUTY AND THE BEAST.

TOP RIGHT: MICHAELA CONSTANCE OF CIRKUS BUSCH.

TOP LEFT: DOREEN DUGAN'S ELEPHANTS AT OLYMPIA.

CENTRE:
LONDON BORN RAY WALKER WITH ONE OF HER TEN LIONS.

RIGHT: EDITH CROCKER REHEARSES HER

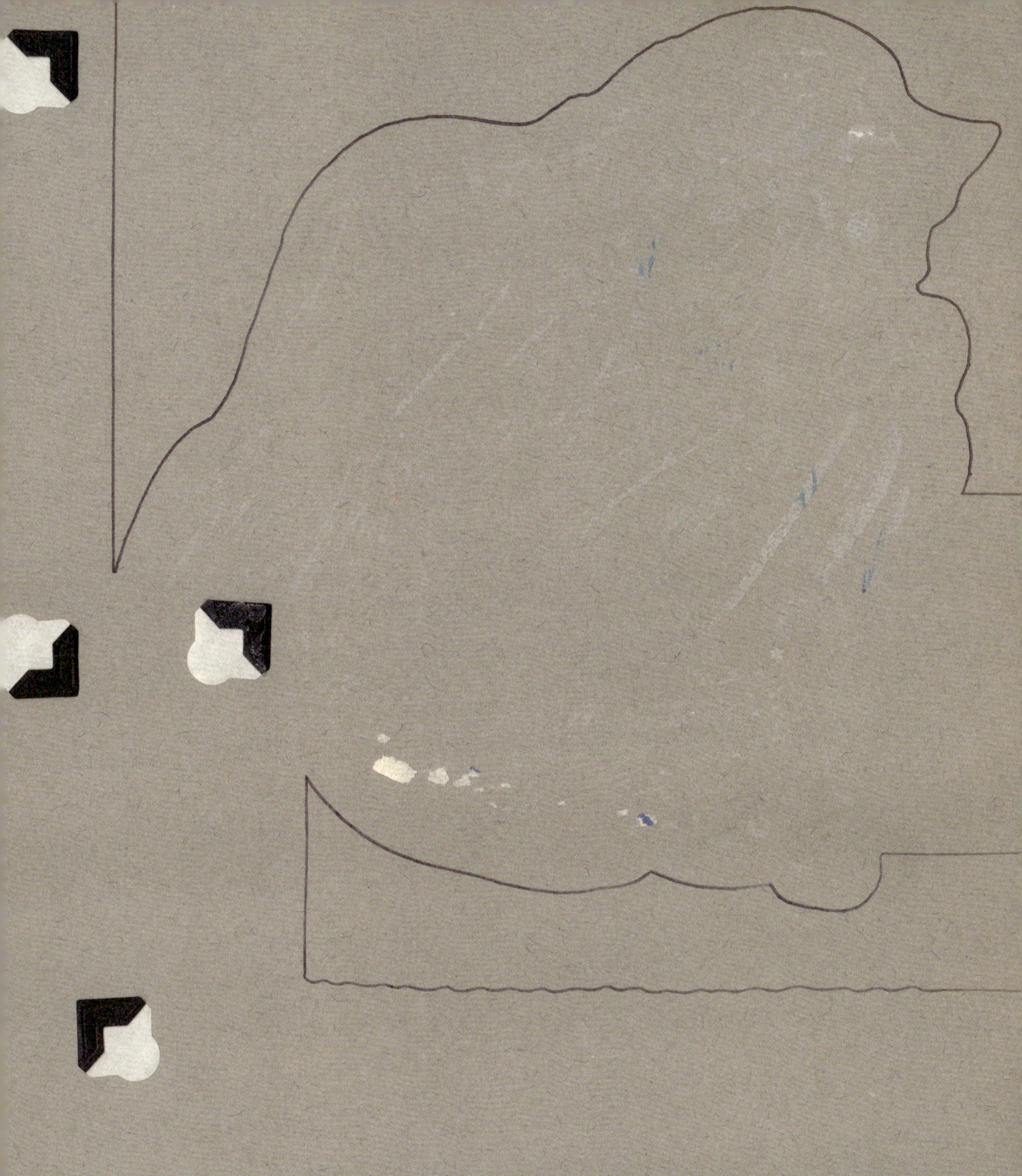

ARS.

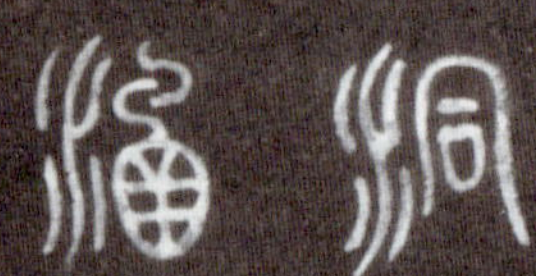

十公分厚碎磚
六種底脚用六
十又九十公分
一種以往分六
混凝土圍及筒
涵洞僅設觀音

挖碎做底脚

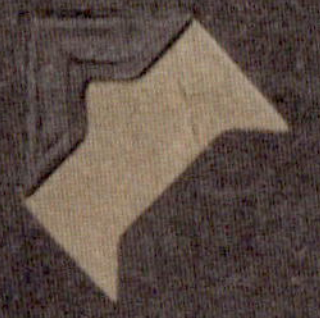
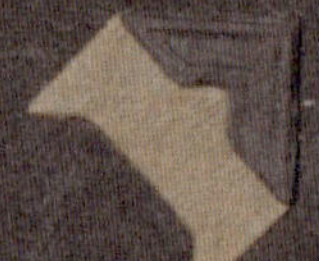
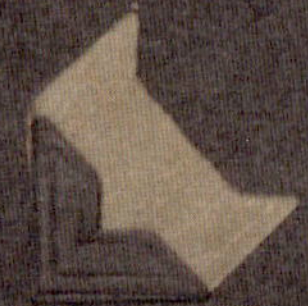
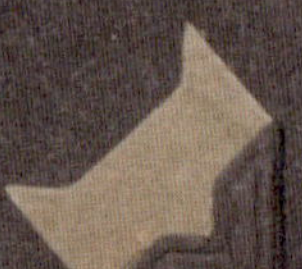

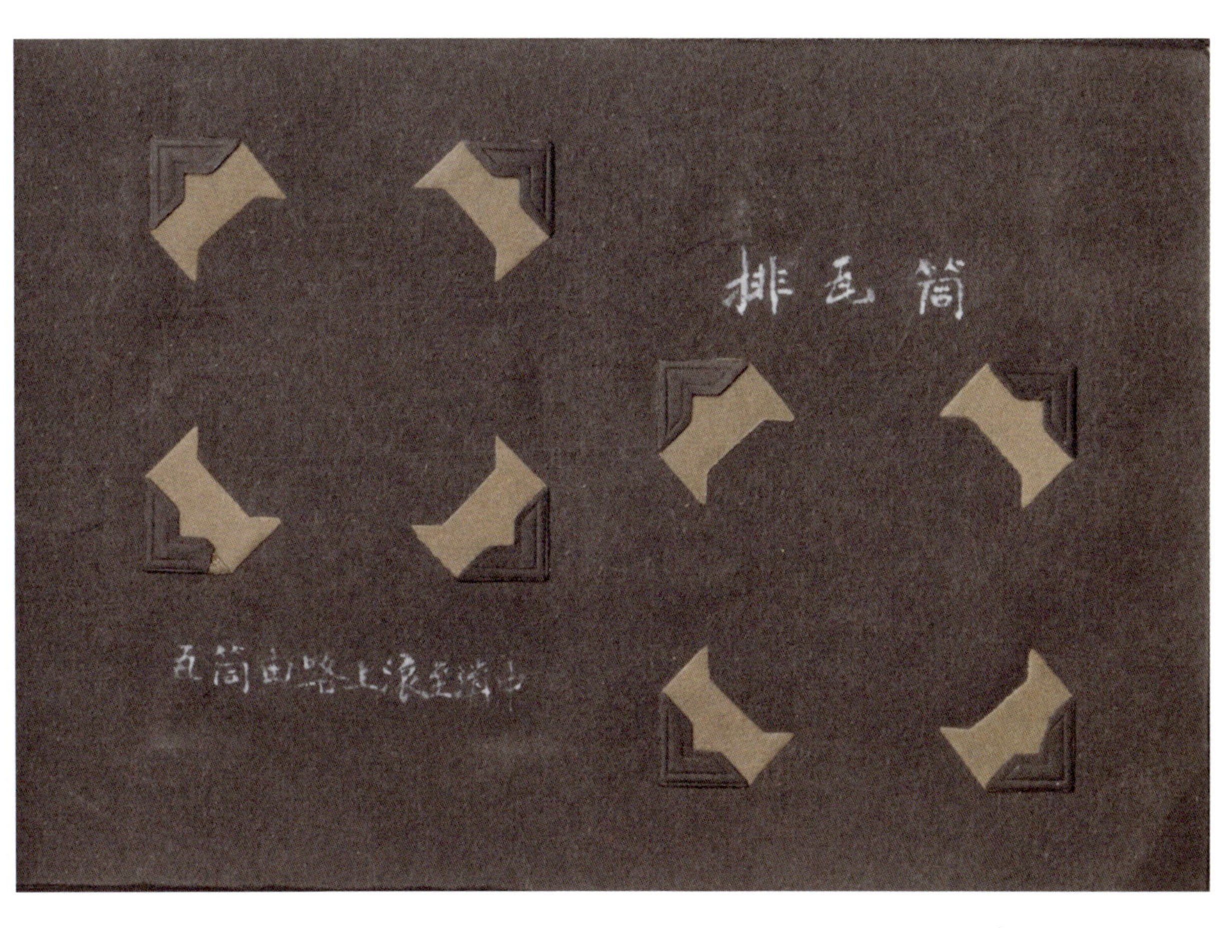
排瓦筒
瓦筒由路上浪至嘴出

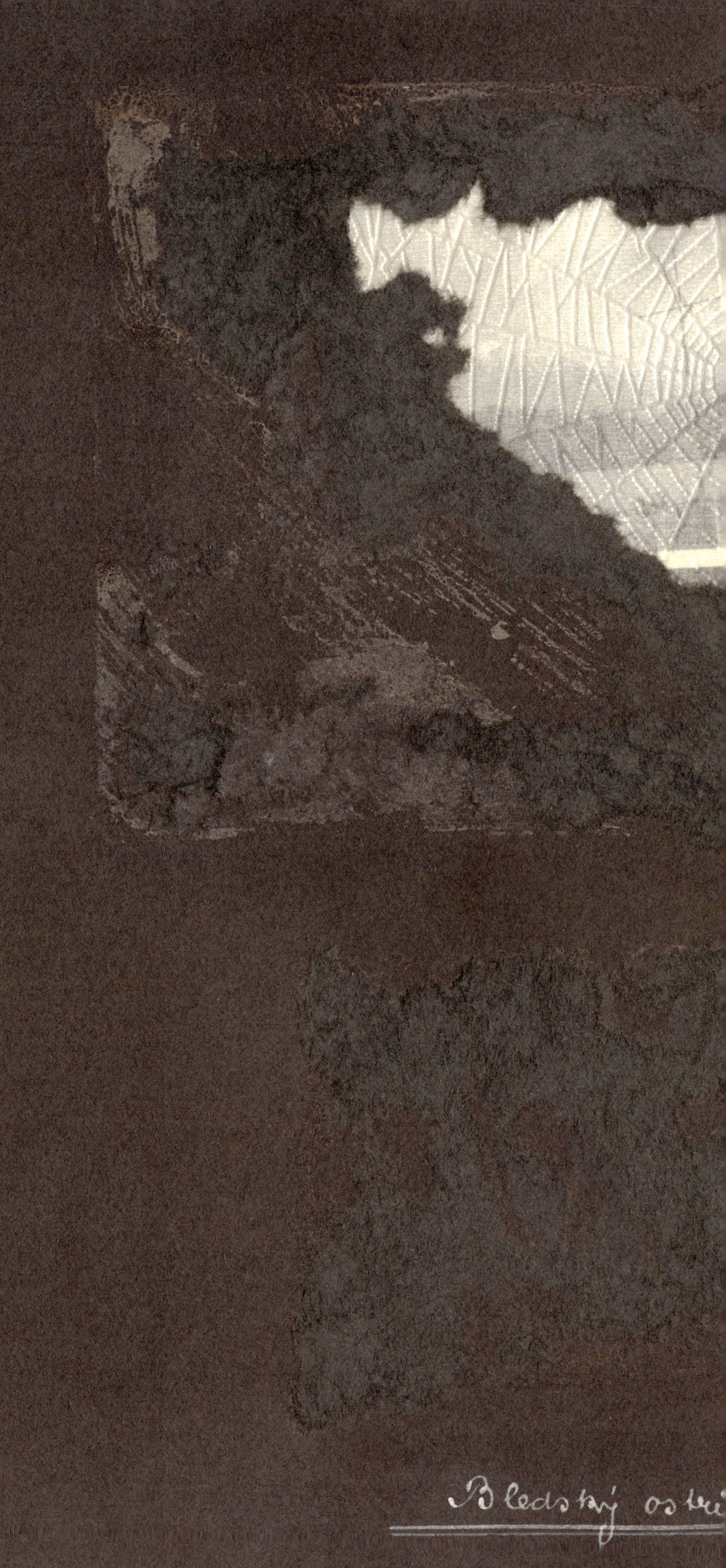
Bledský

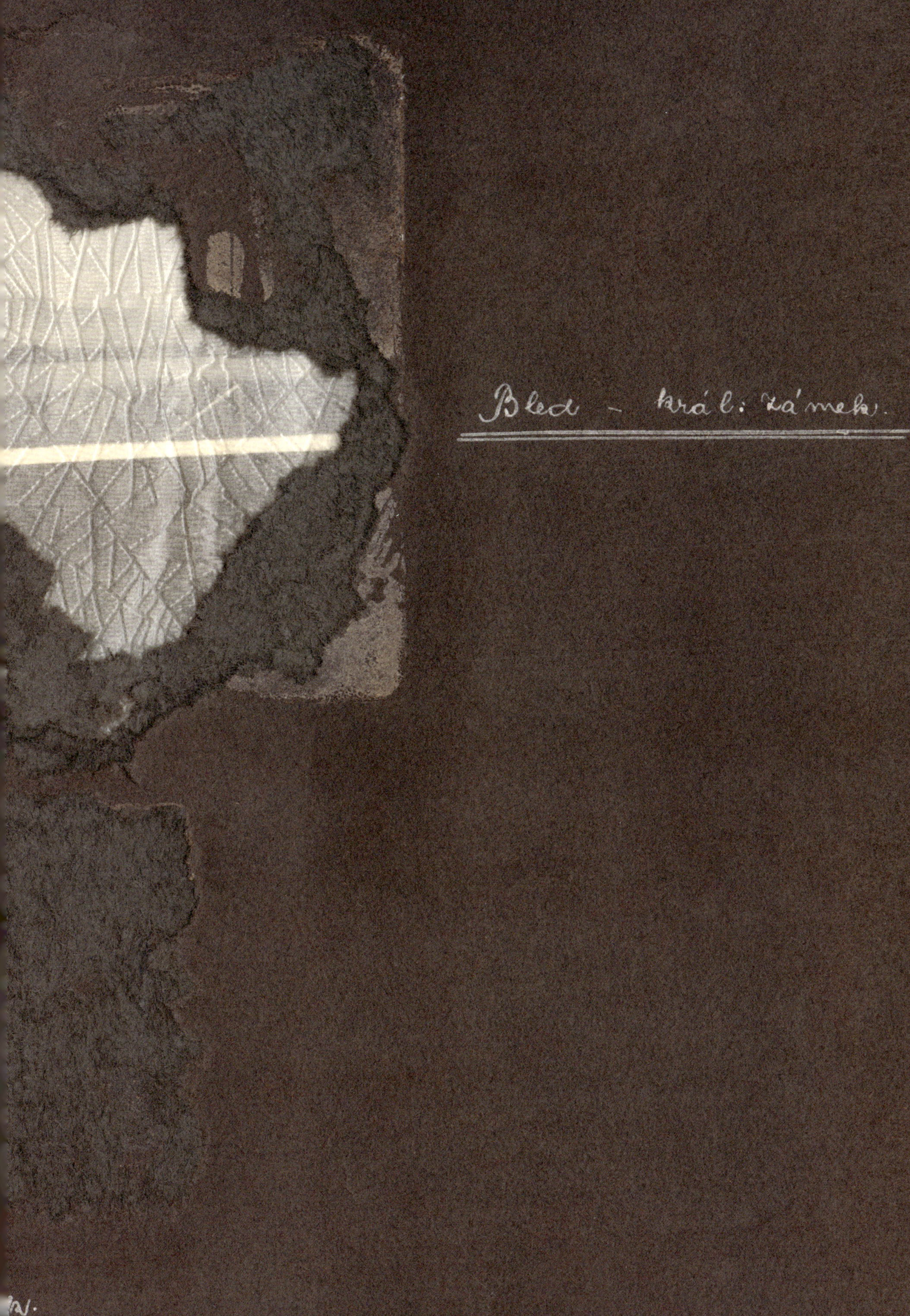

Bled - král: zámek.

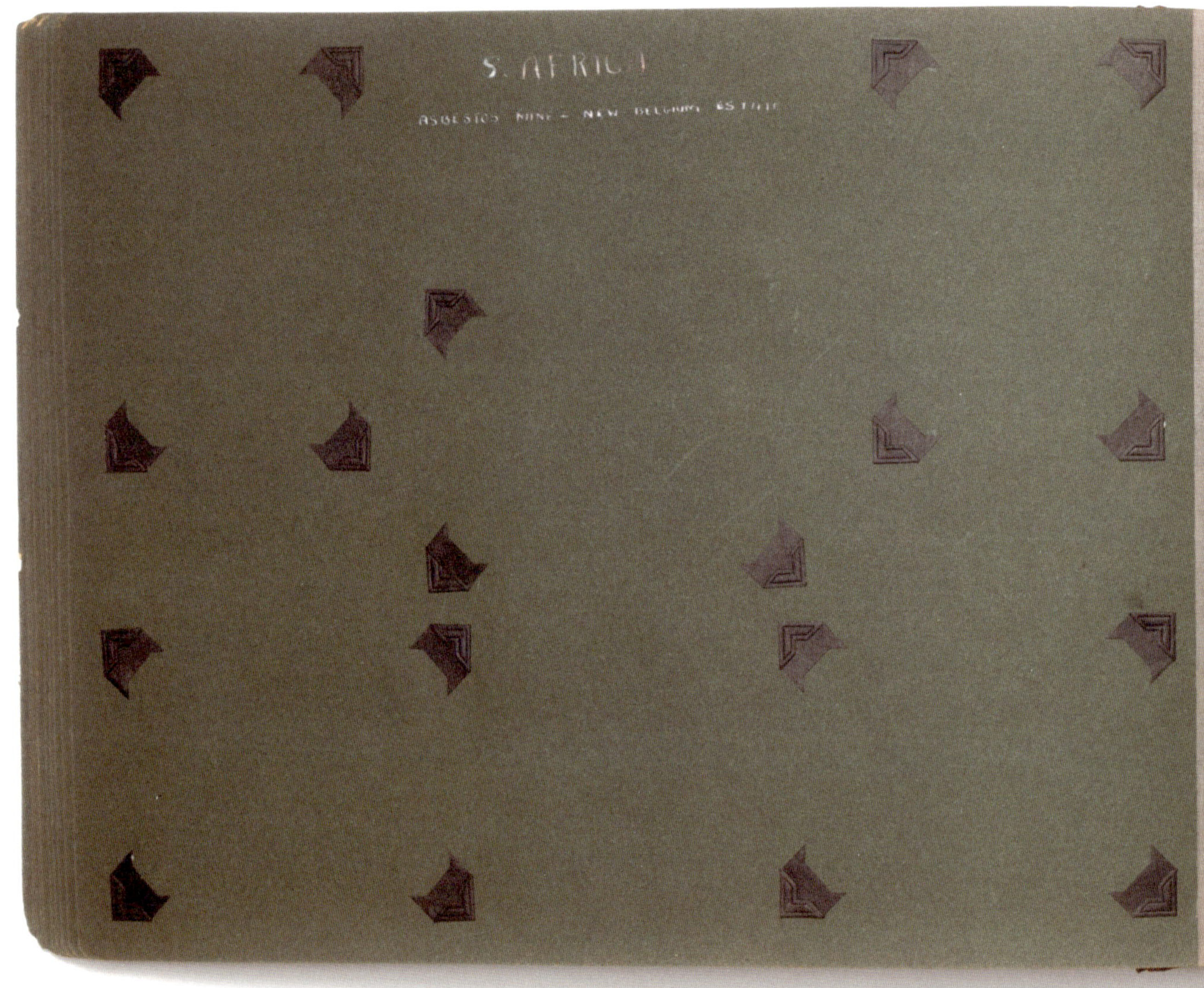
S. AFRICA
ASBESTOS MINE – NEW BELGIUM ESTATE

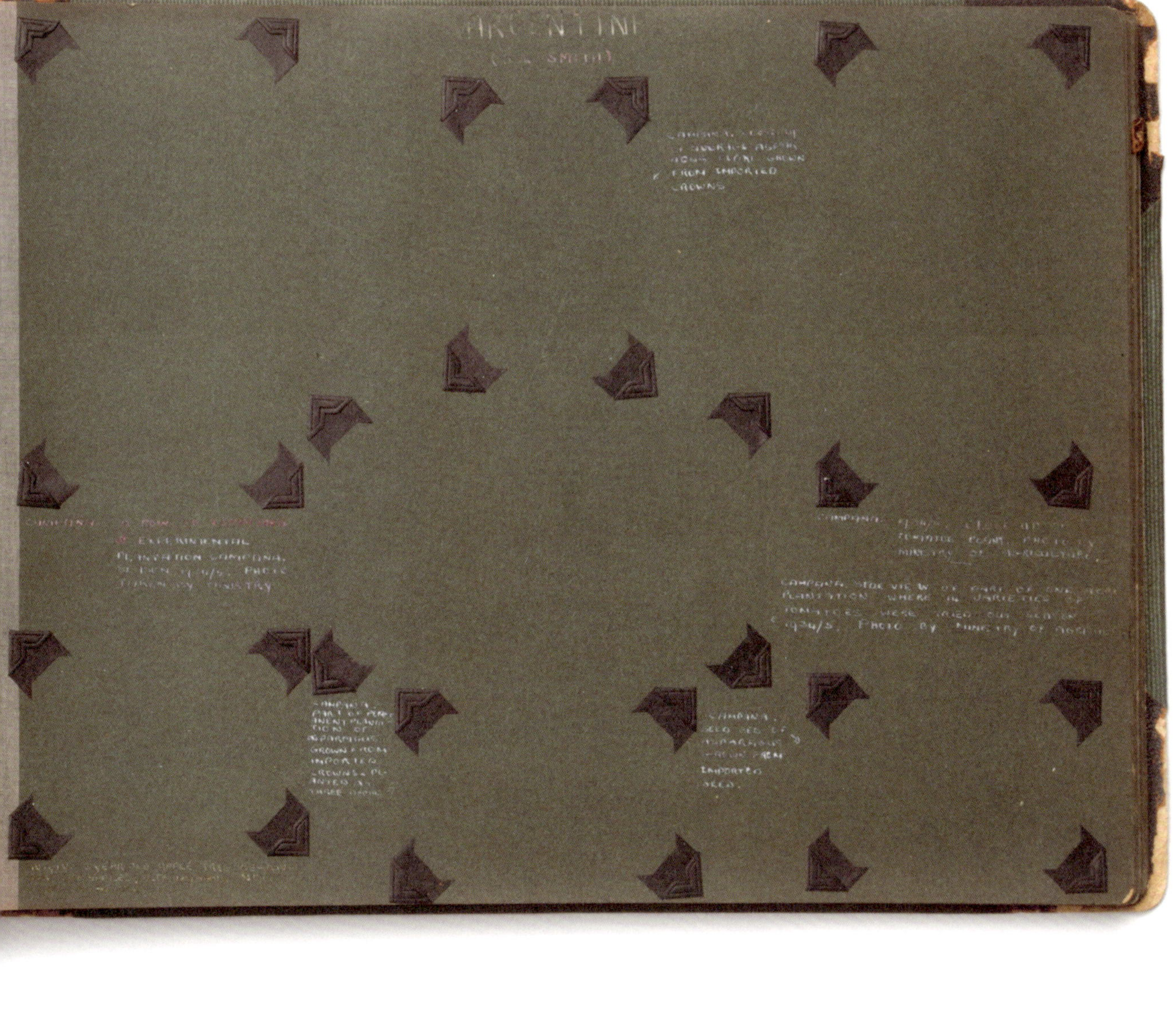

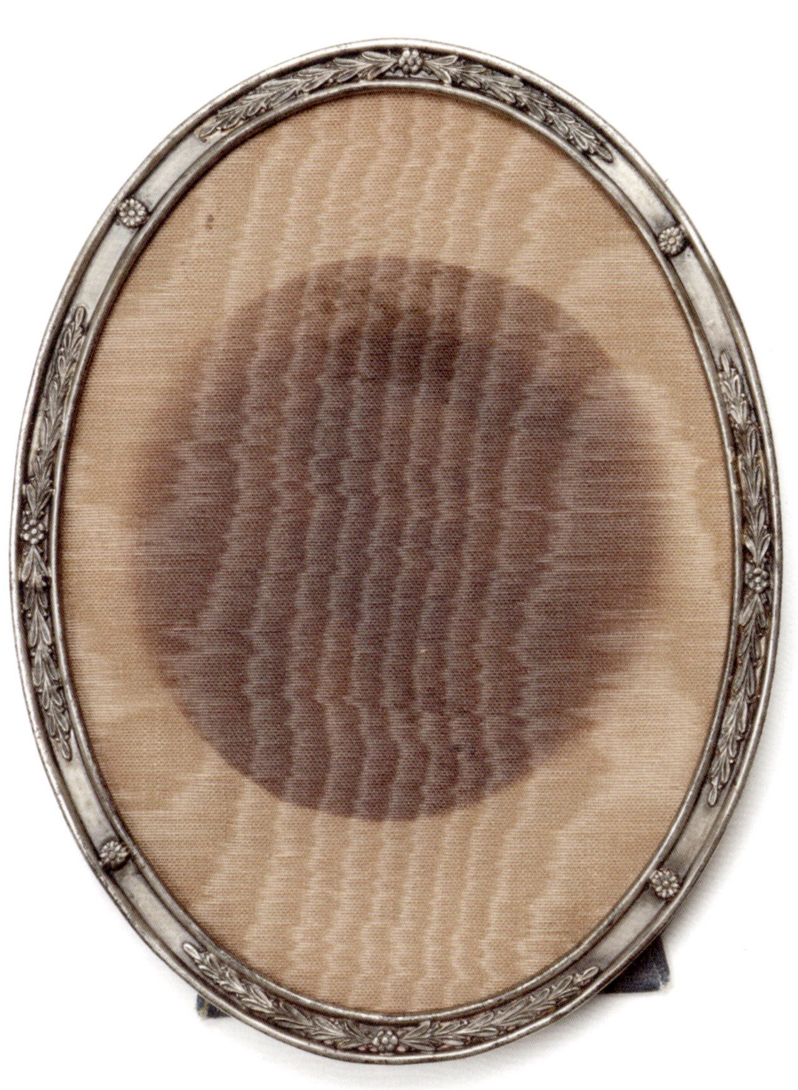

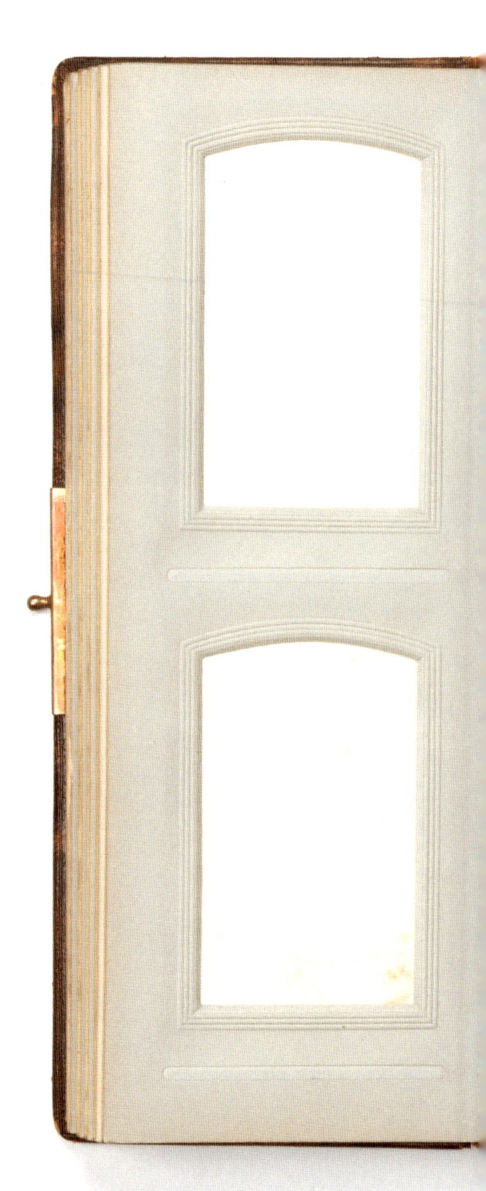

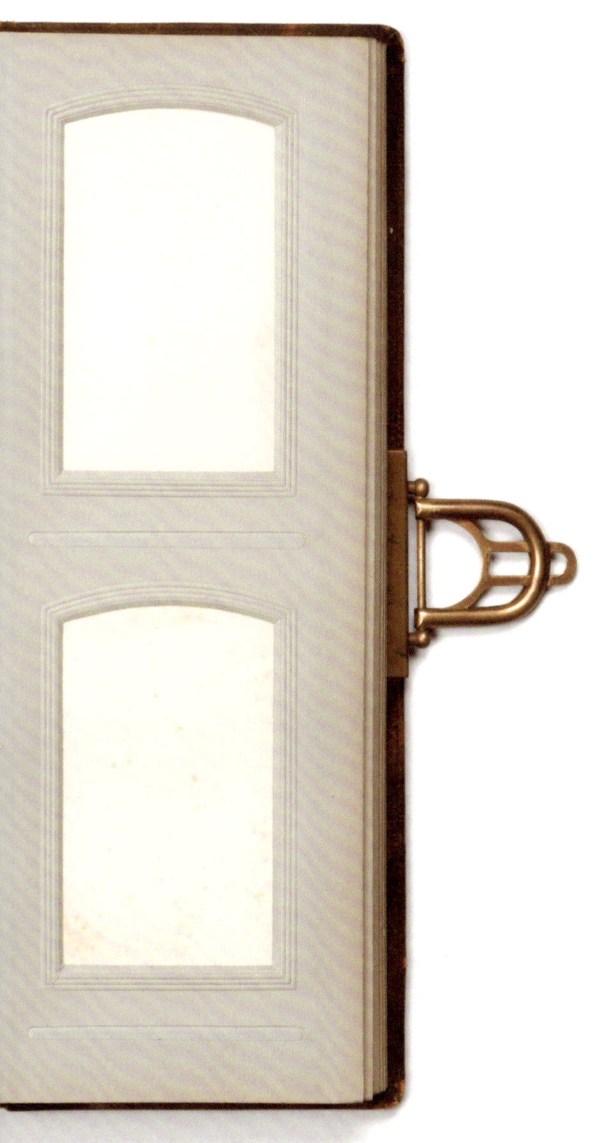

195

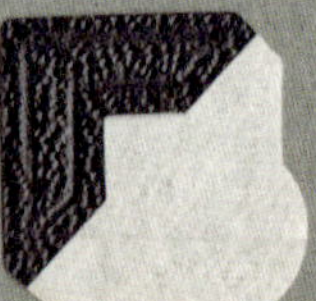
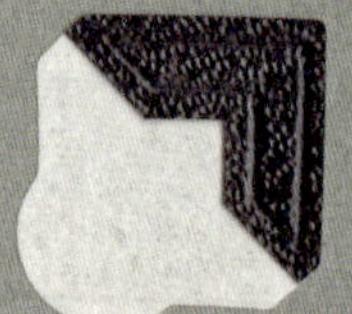
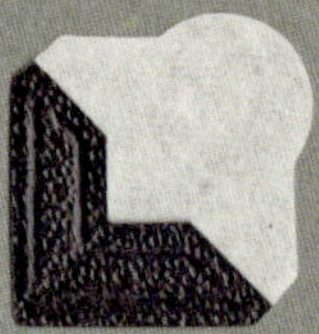
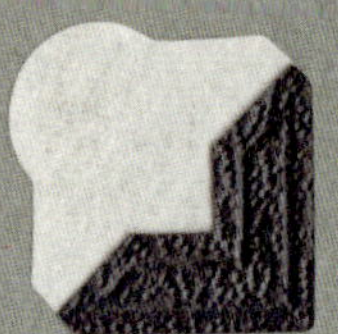

UGHTER PANTOMIME

BOOTS"

67

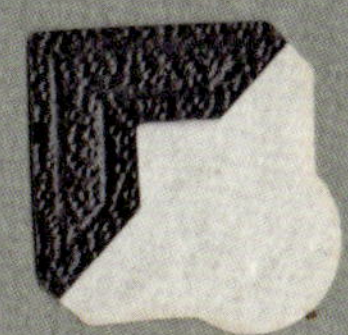
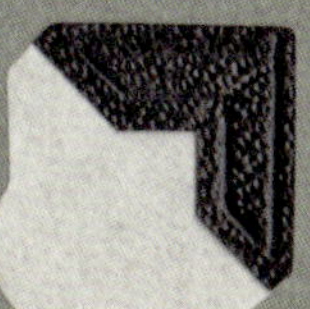
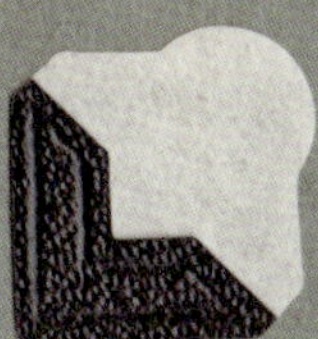
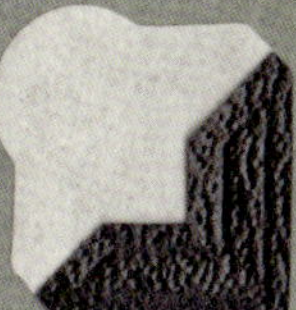

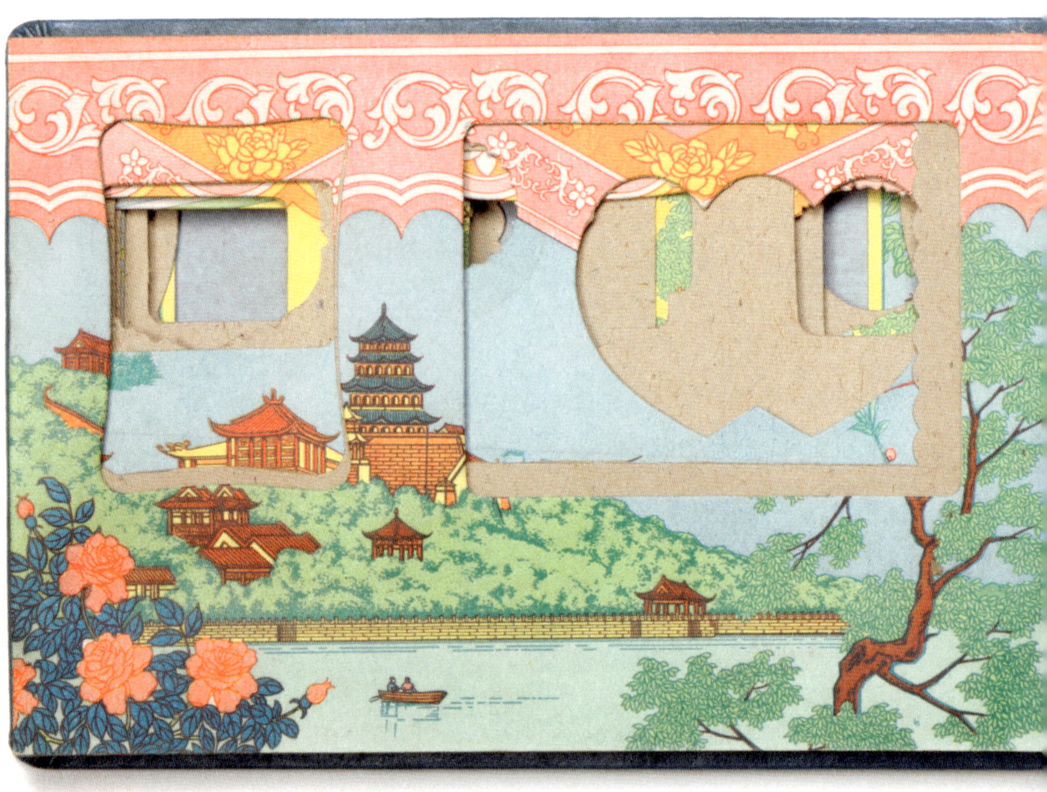

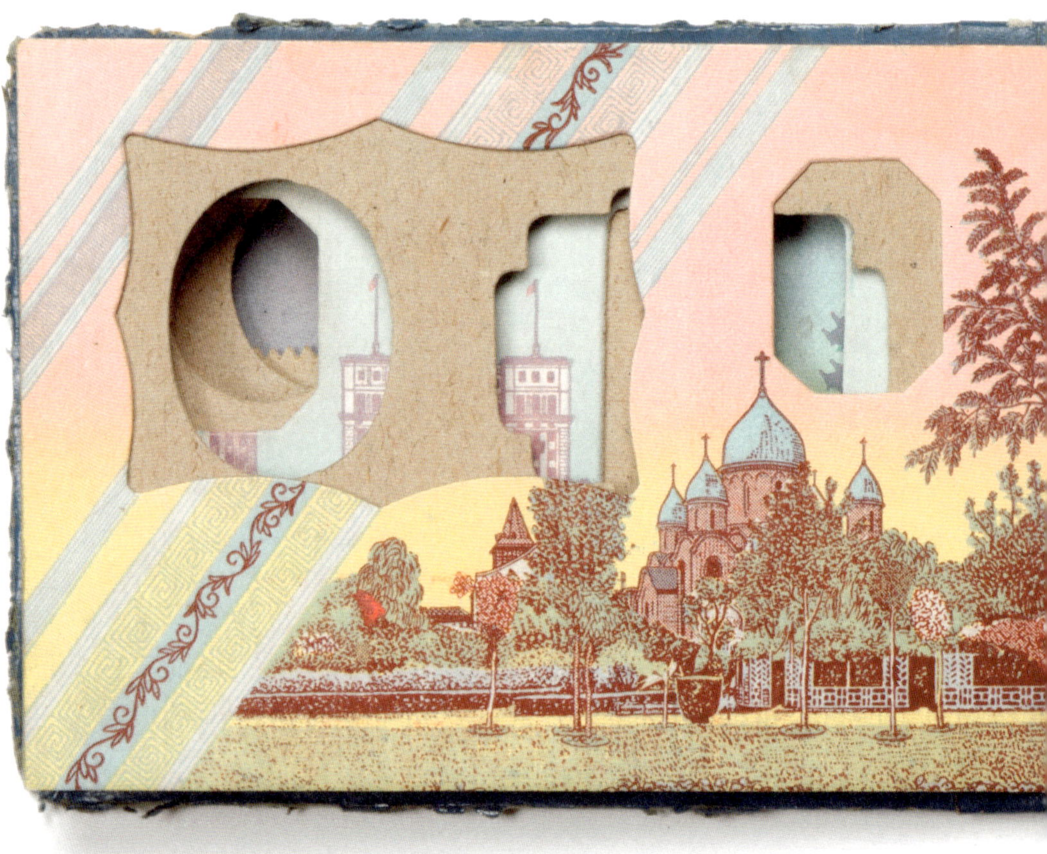

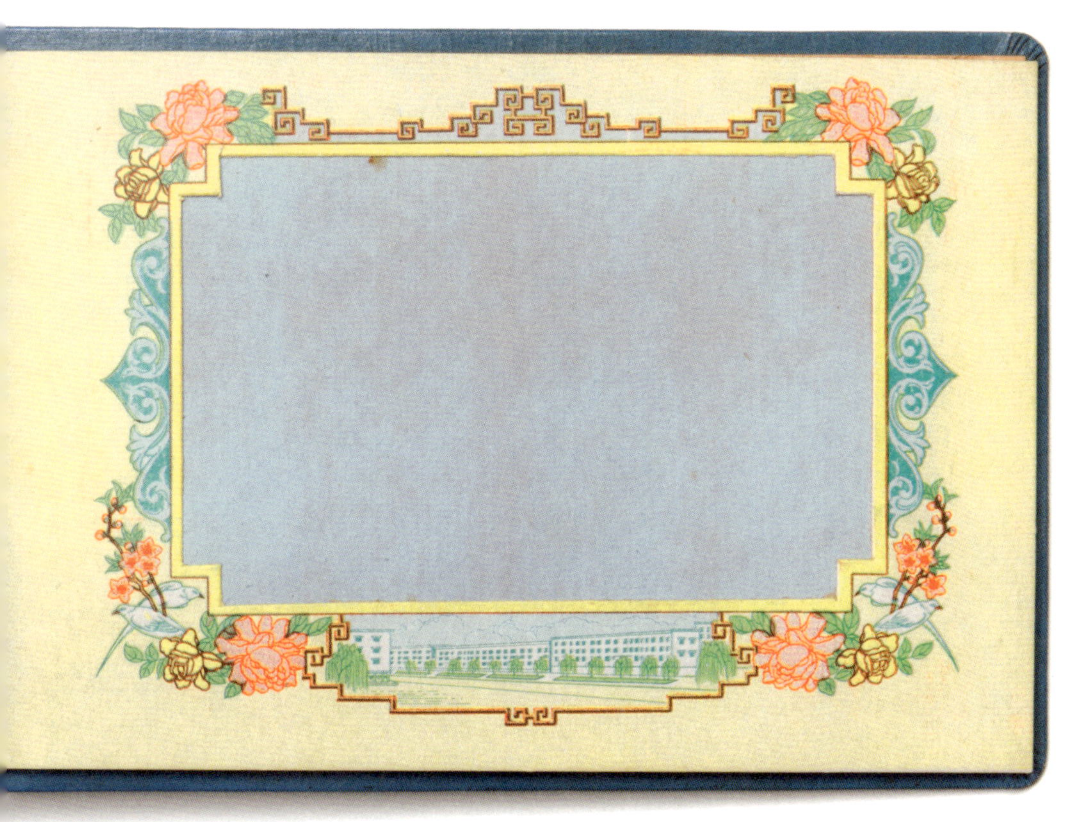

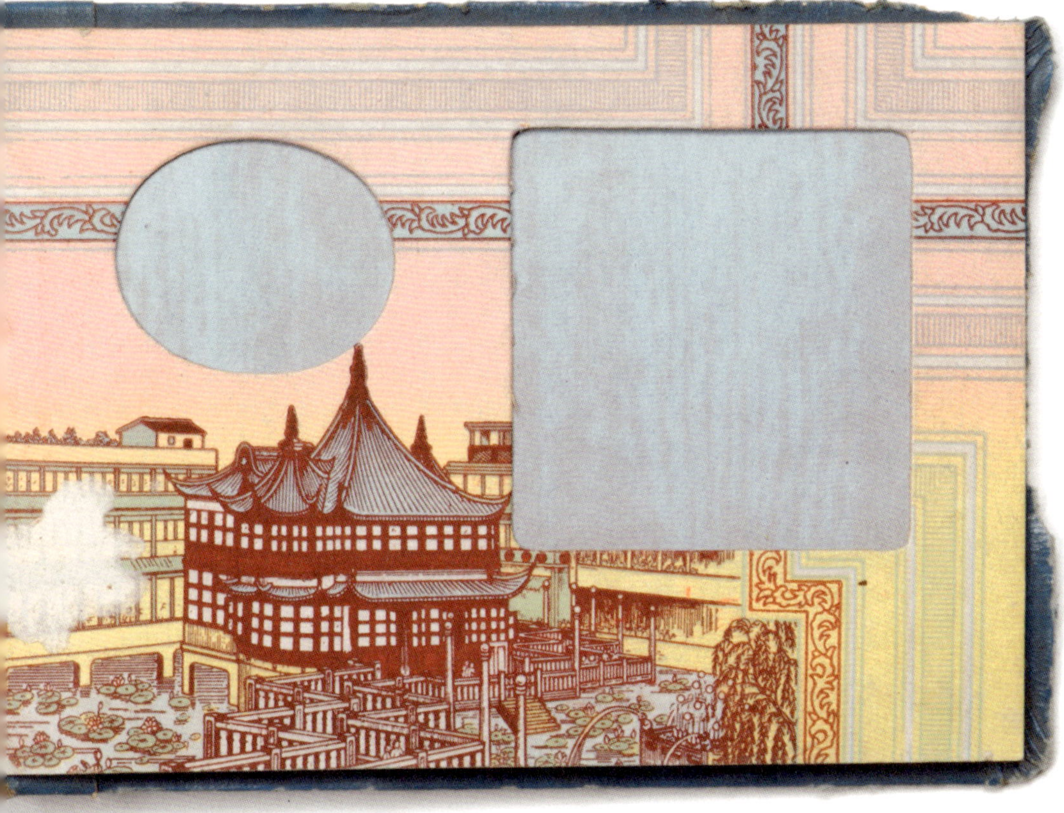

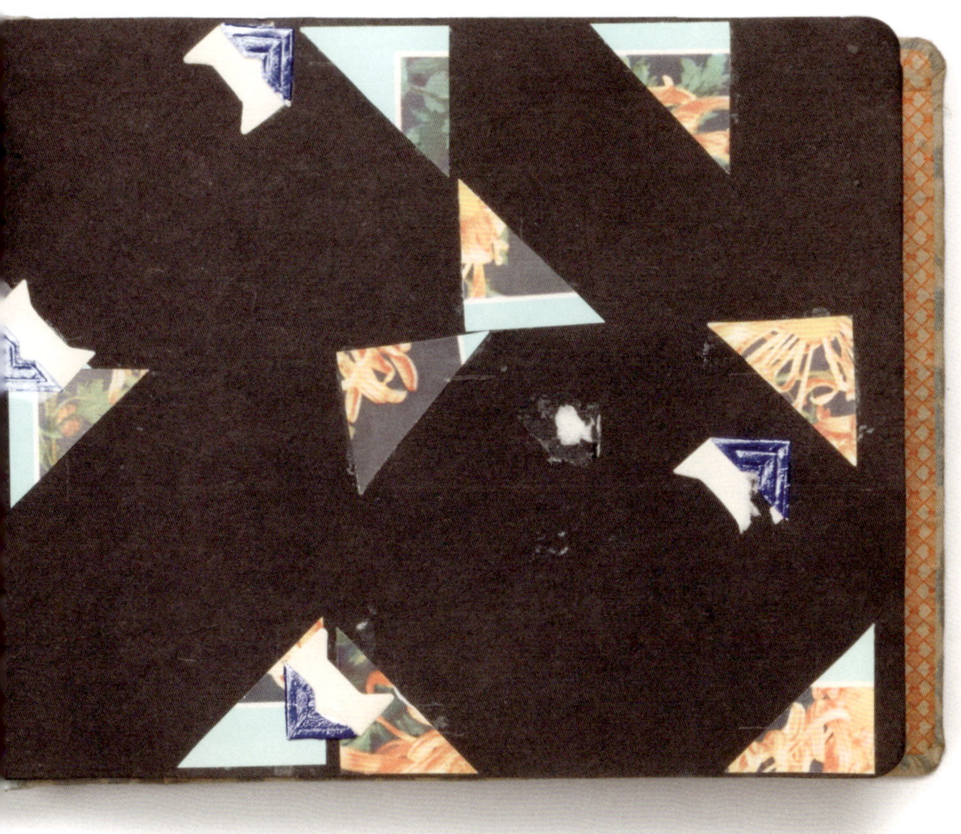

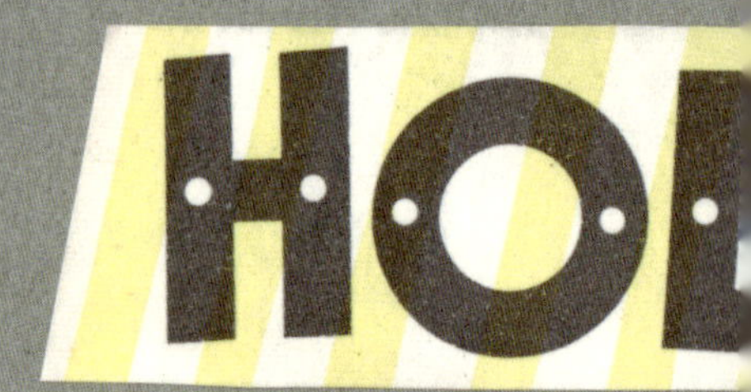

Frankie Vaughan g

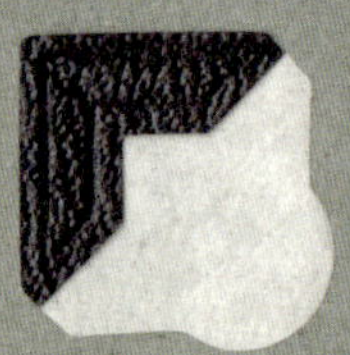

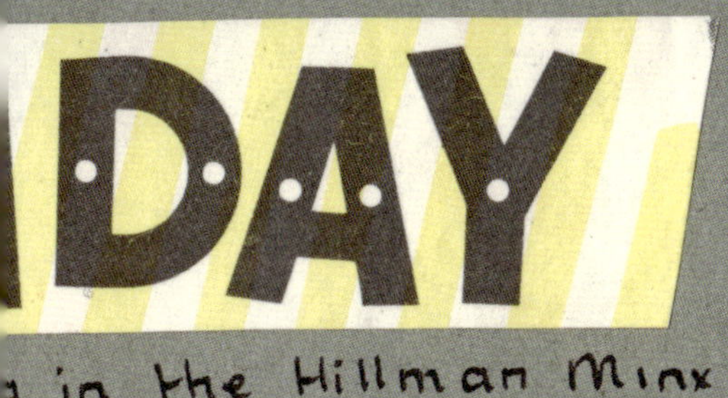

g in the Hillman Minx.

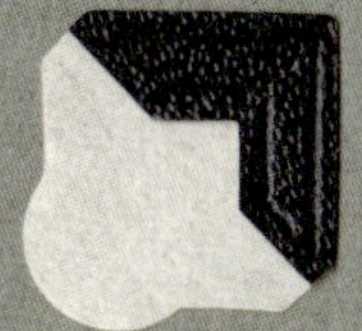

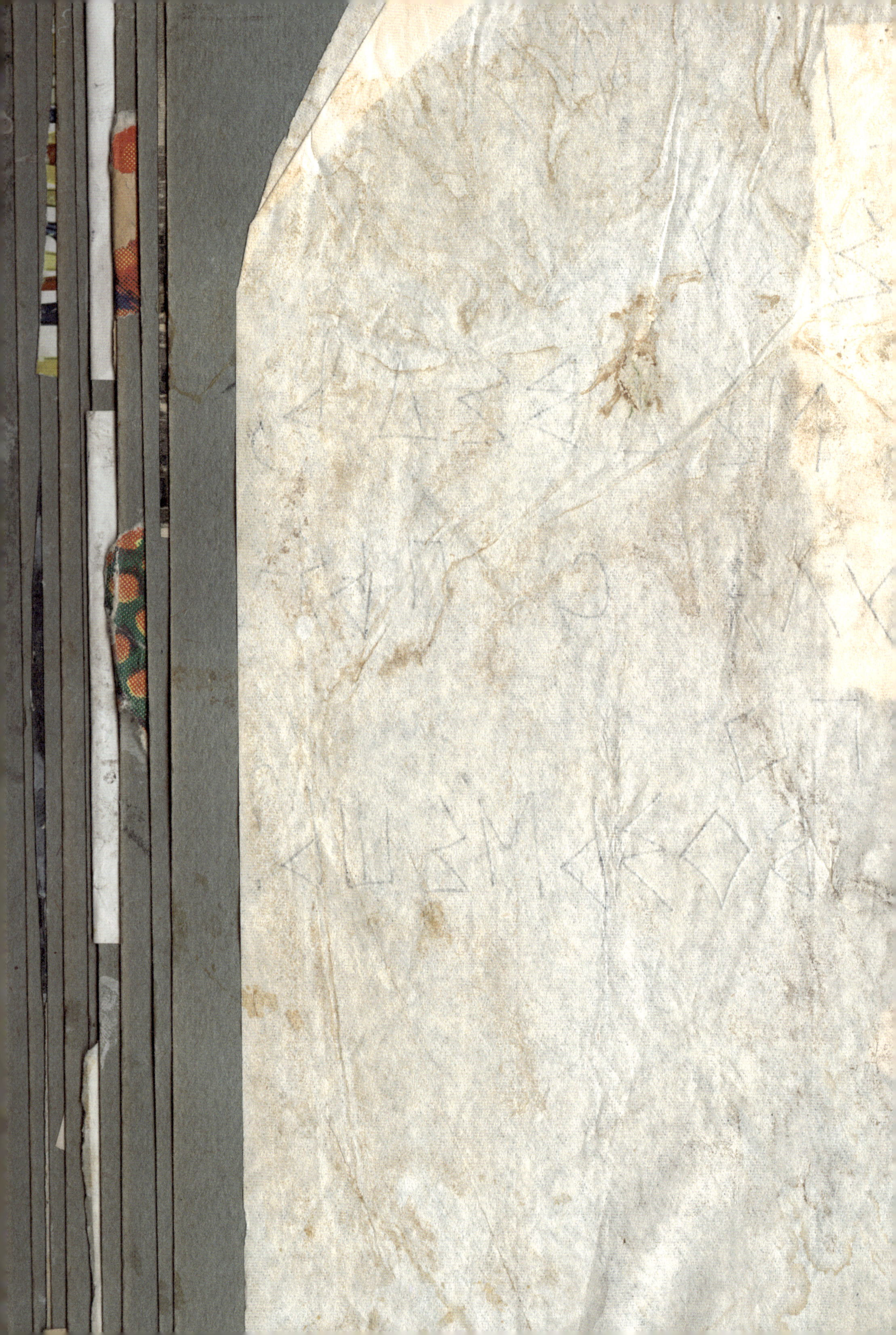

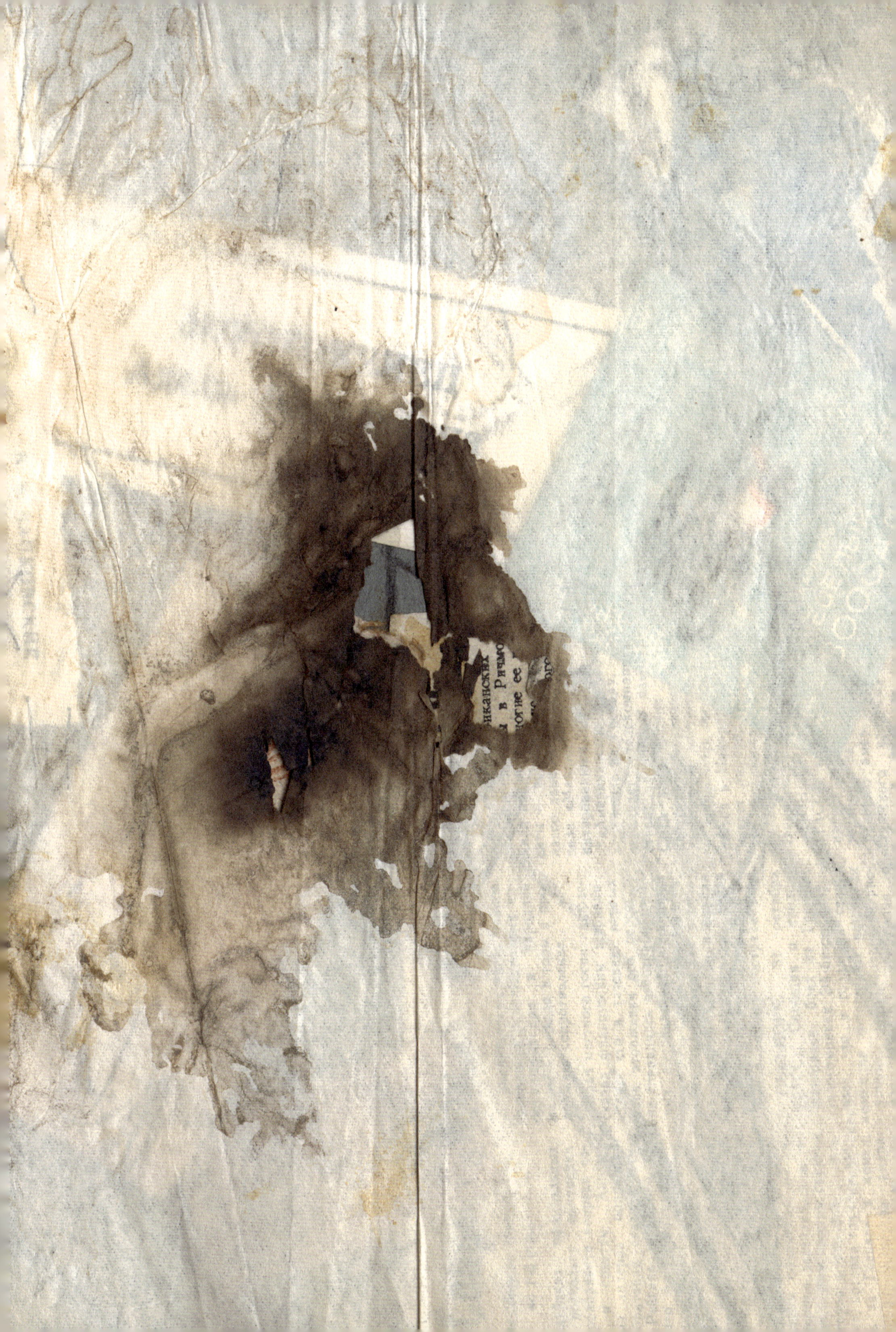

2/3

Winkenhurst. September 9th 06
Mary. Cynthia. Carlo. Stella. Alise. May
Pip Nick.

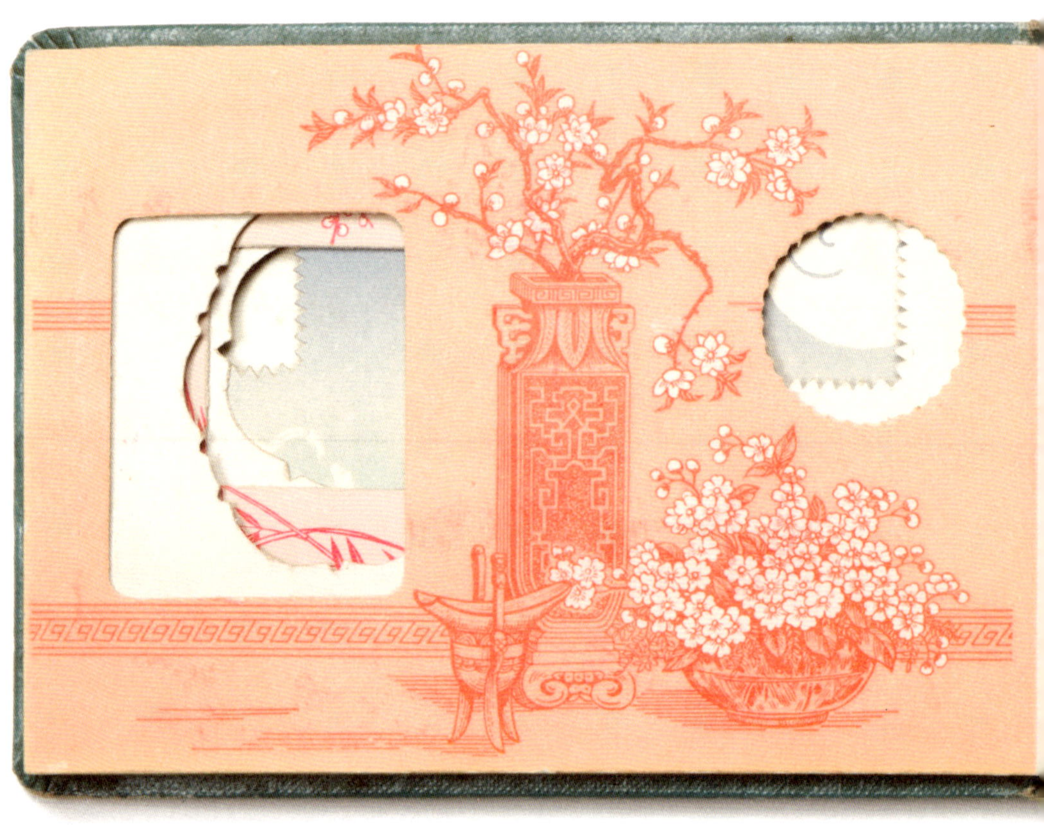

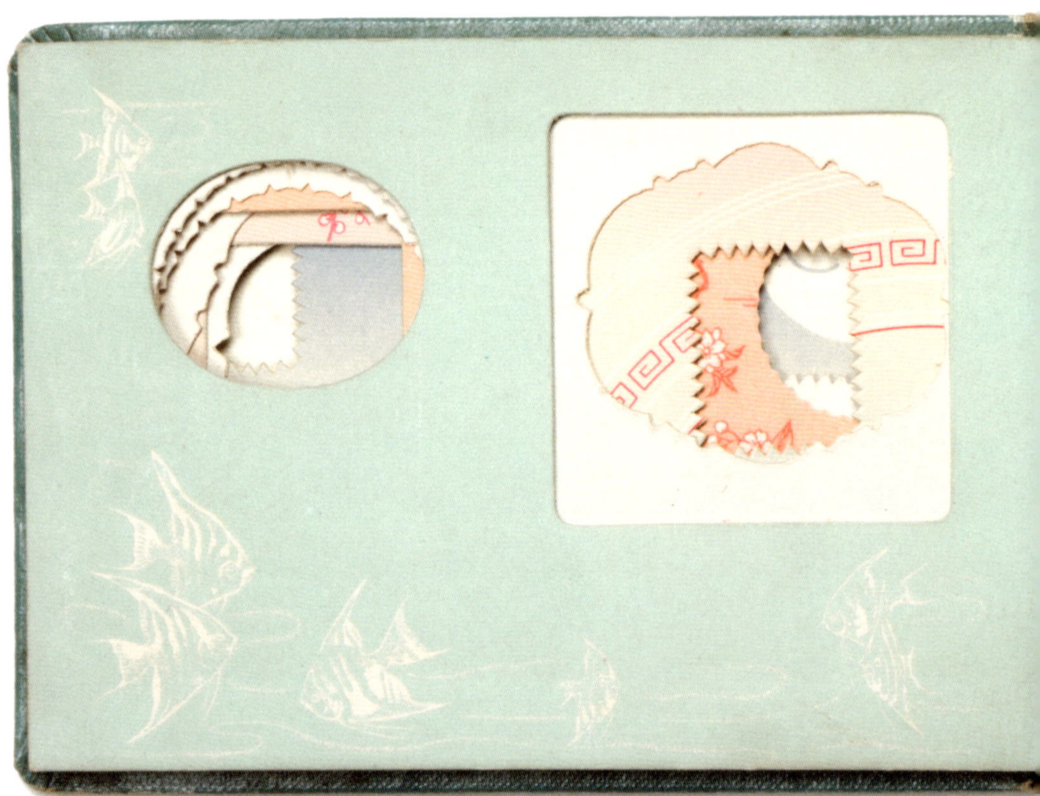

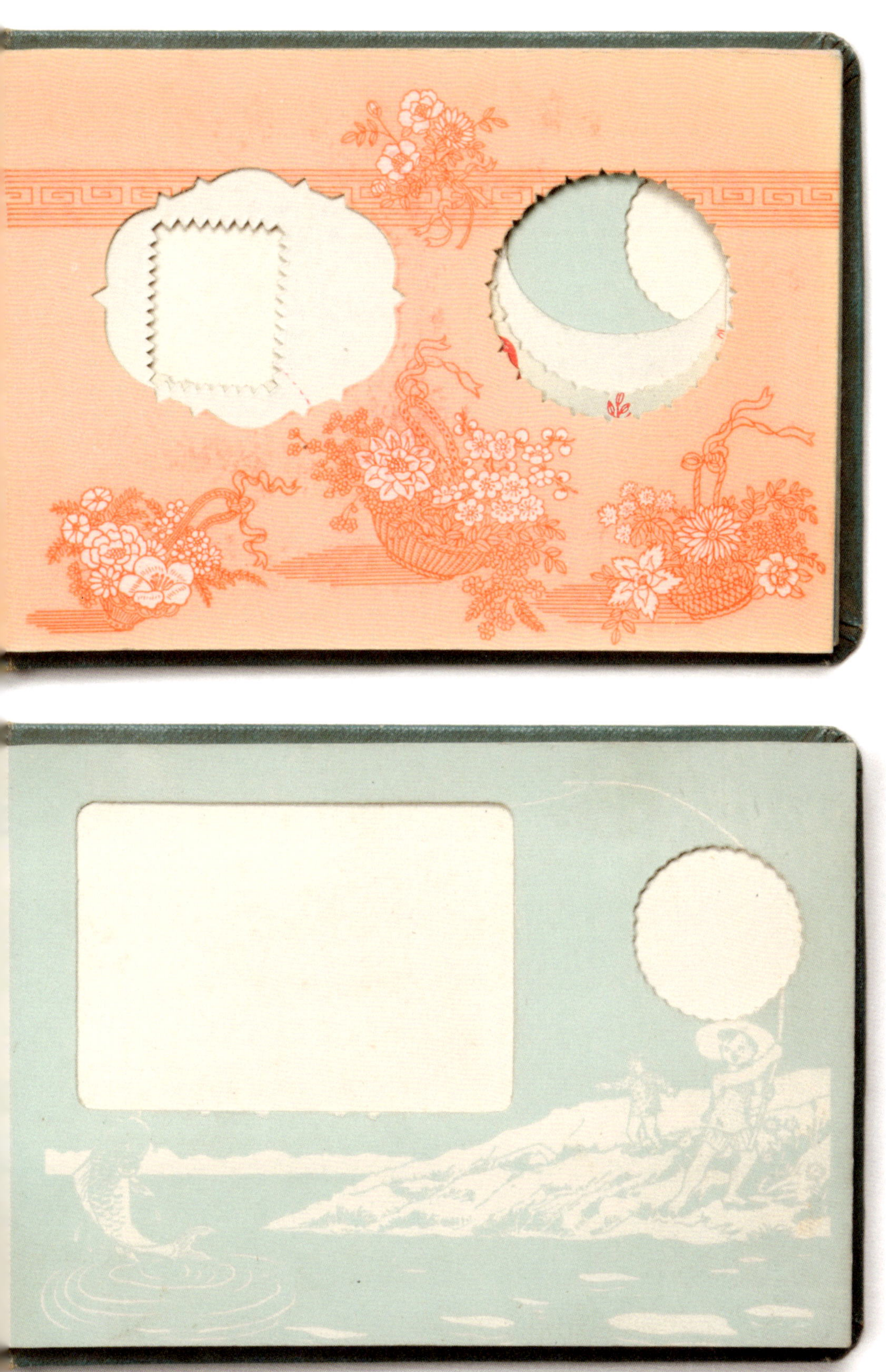

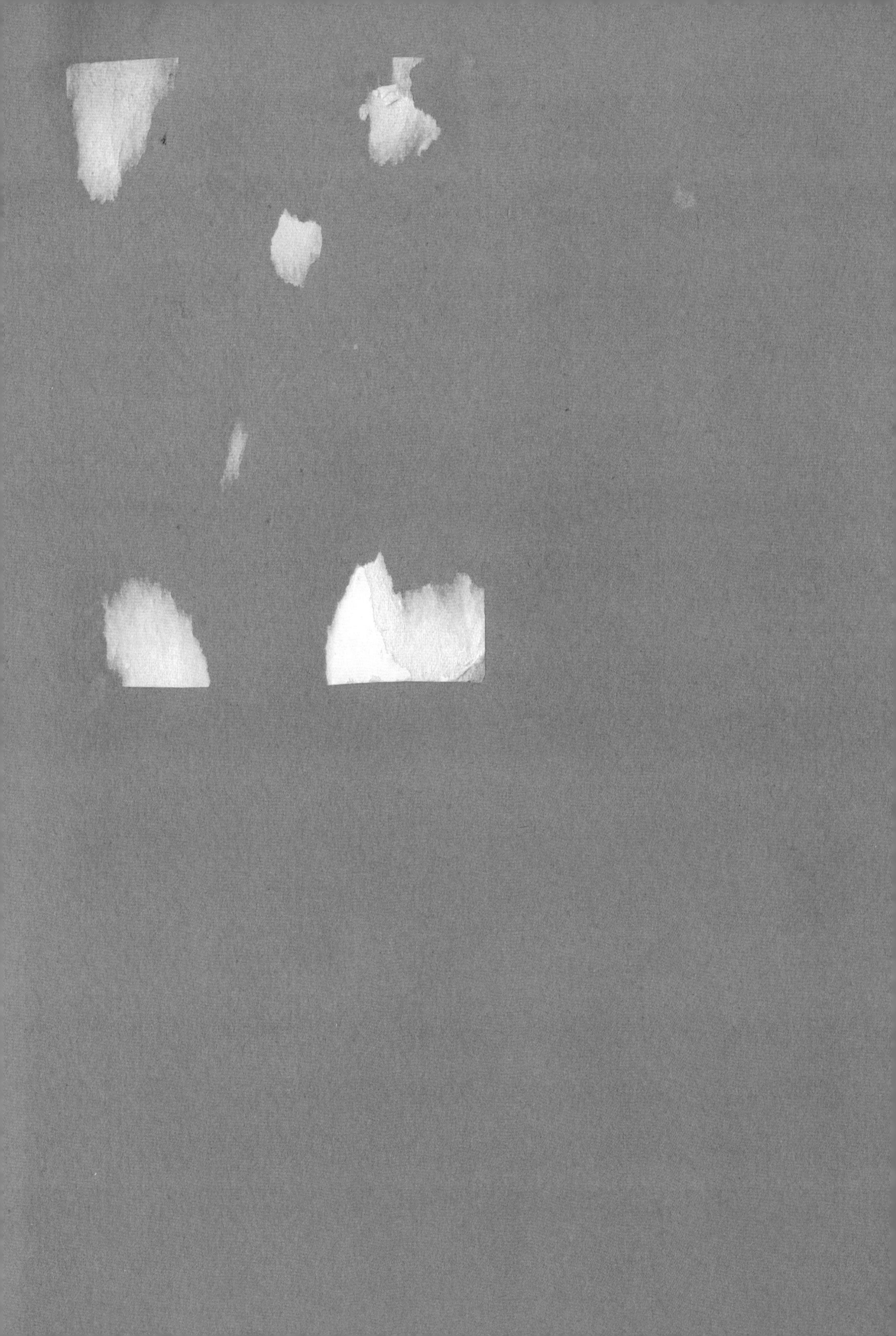

ADOLPH

ackowledges his applause in the manner befitting a Super-Star,

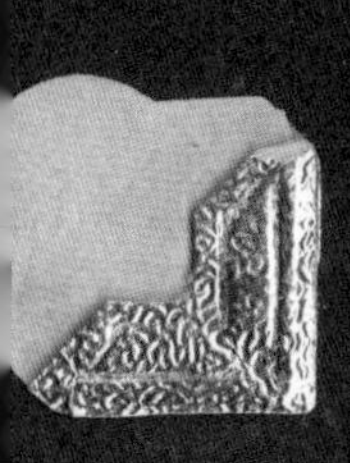

französi

Rote-Kreuz-Schwestern helfen . . .

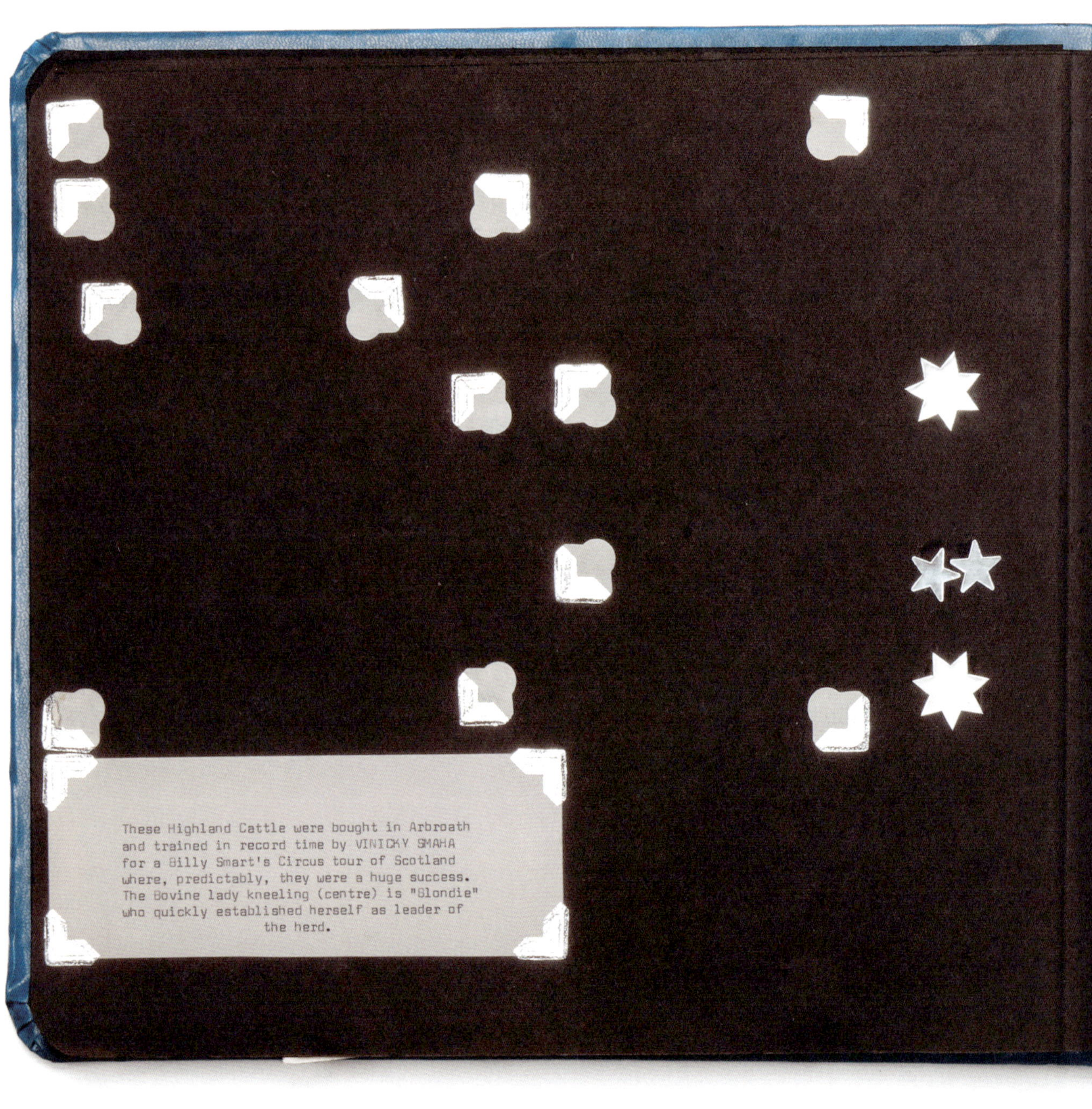
These Highland Cattle were bought in Arbroath
and trained in record time by VINICKY SMAHA
for a Billy Smart's Circus tour of Scotland
where, predictably, they were a huge success.
The Bovine lady kneeling (centre) is "Blondie"
who quickly established herself as leader of
the herd.

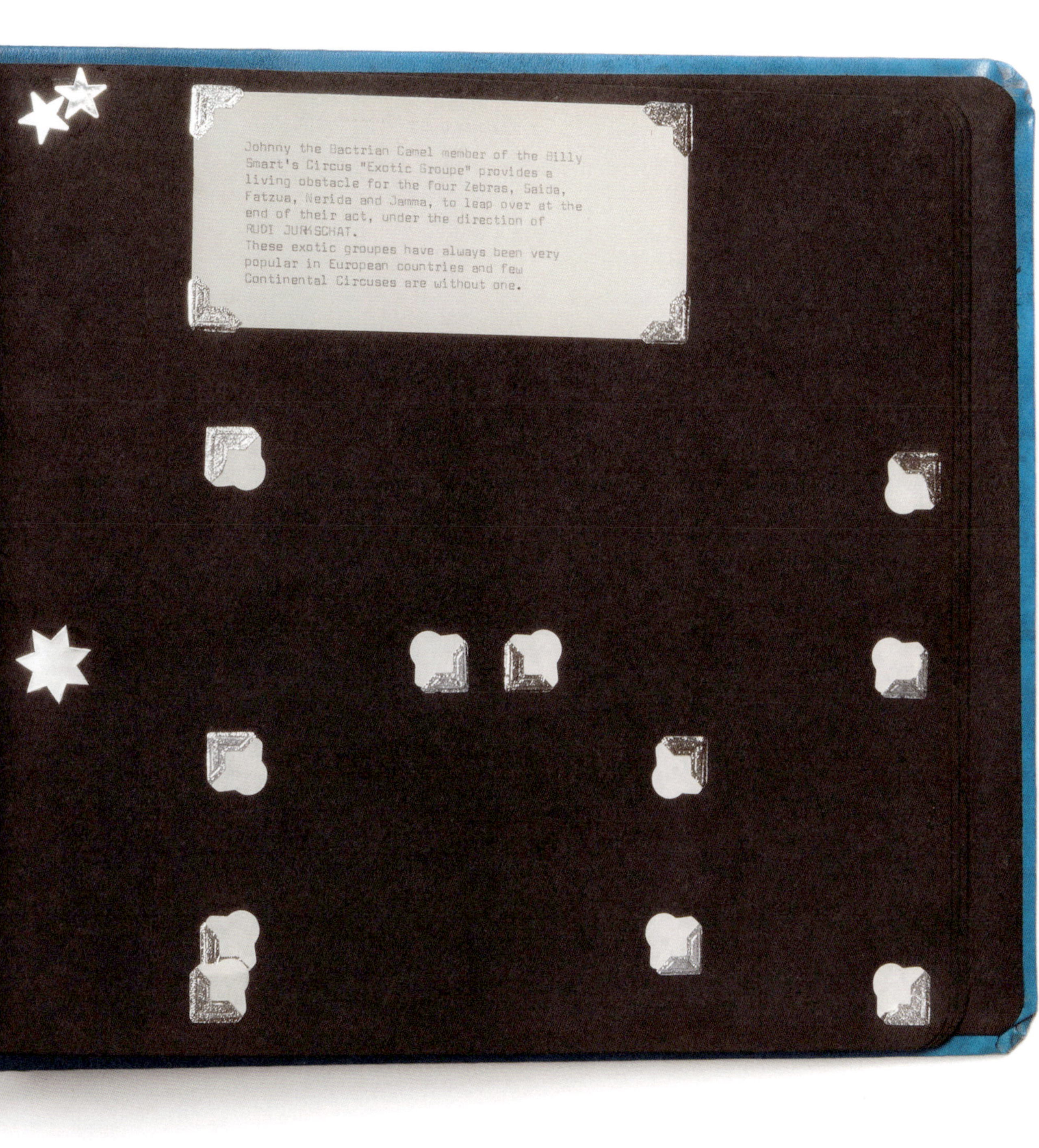
Johnny the Bactrian Camel member of the Billy Smart's Circus "Exotic Groupe" provides a living obstacle for the four Zebras, Saida, Fatzua, Nerida and Jamma, to leap over at the end of their act, under the direction of RUDI JURKSCHAT.
These exotic groupes have always been very popular in European countries and few Continental Circuses are without one.

Opouštíme Crikvenici ve čtvrtek 6. září o 6. hod. večer „Prestolo-
nasljednikem Petarem" okolo Bašky na Ráb. (v 8 h. večer.)

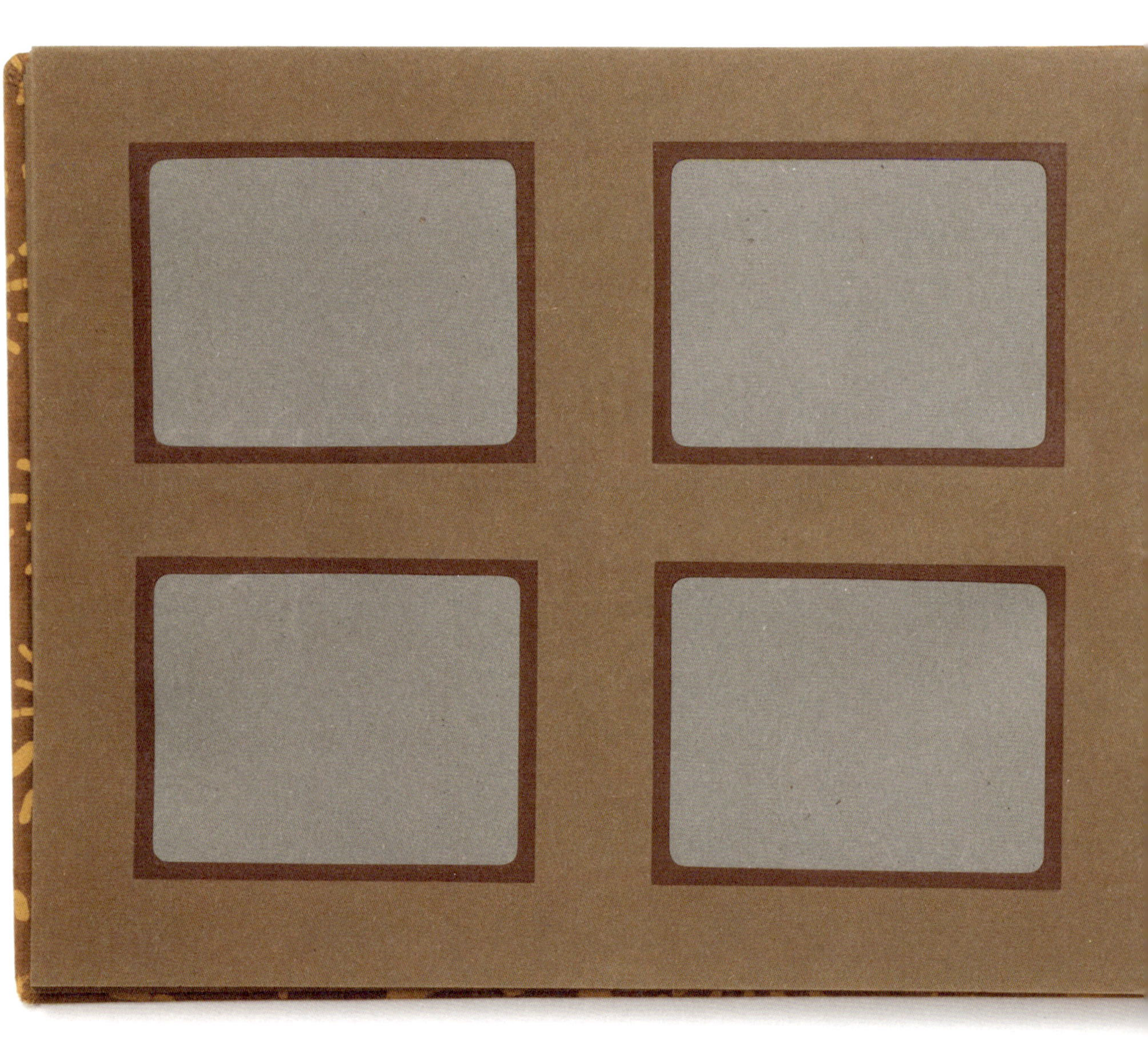

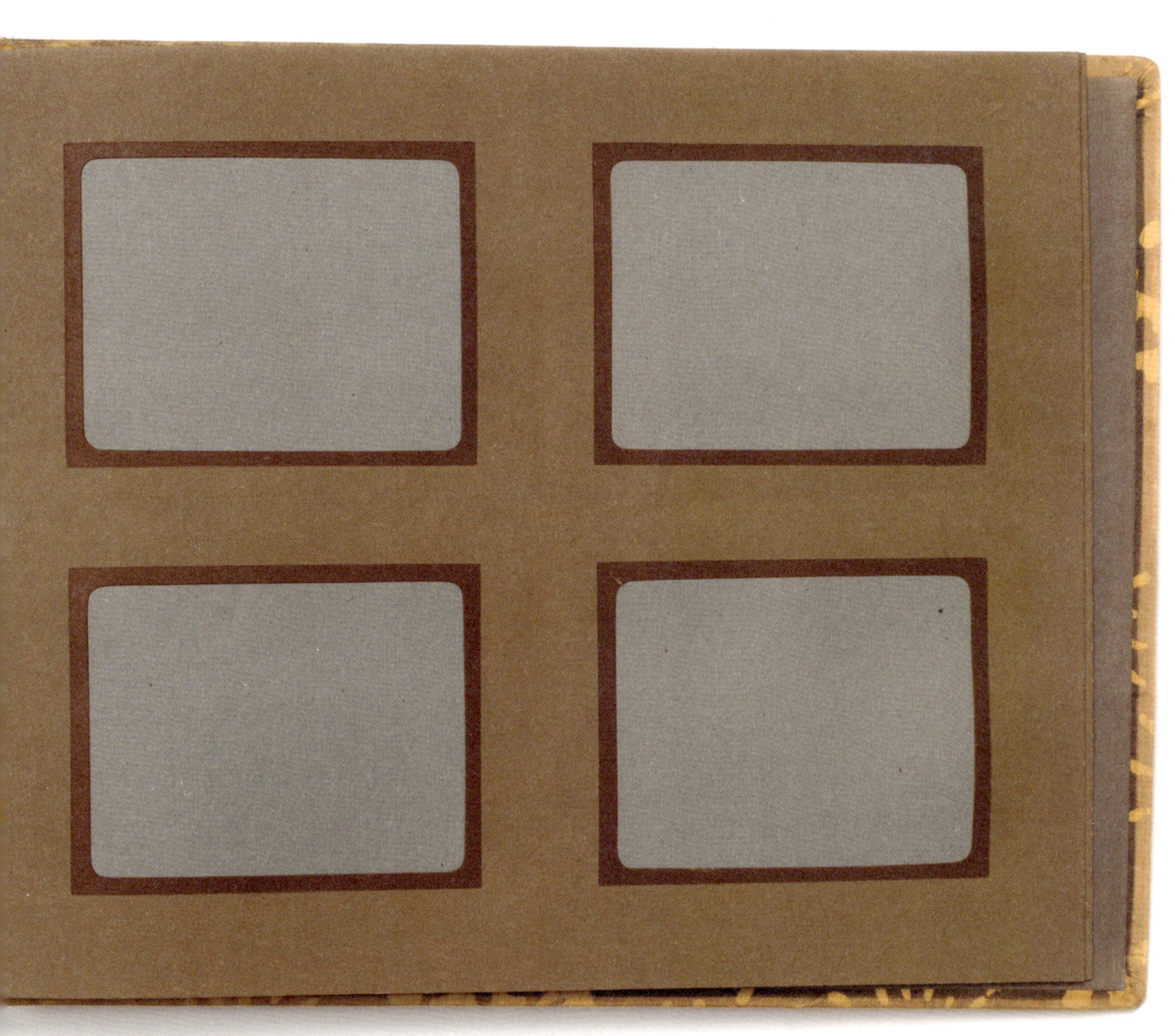

Hauptmann Franke

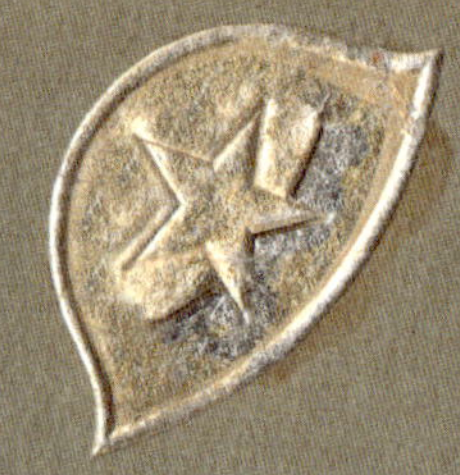

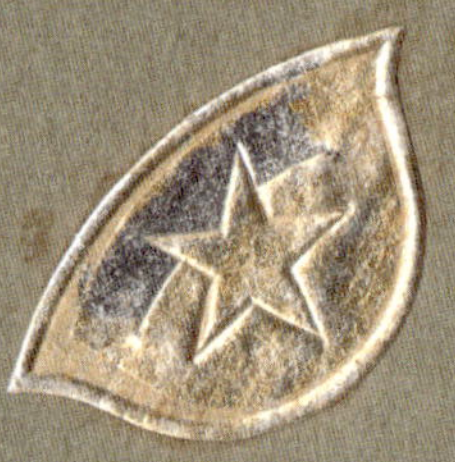

la grand halte
un bon coup.

déjeuner sur le pouce
la gamelle.

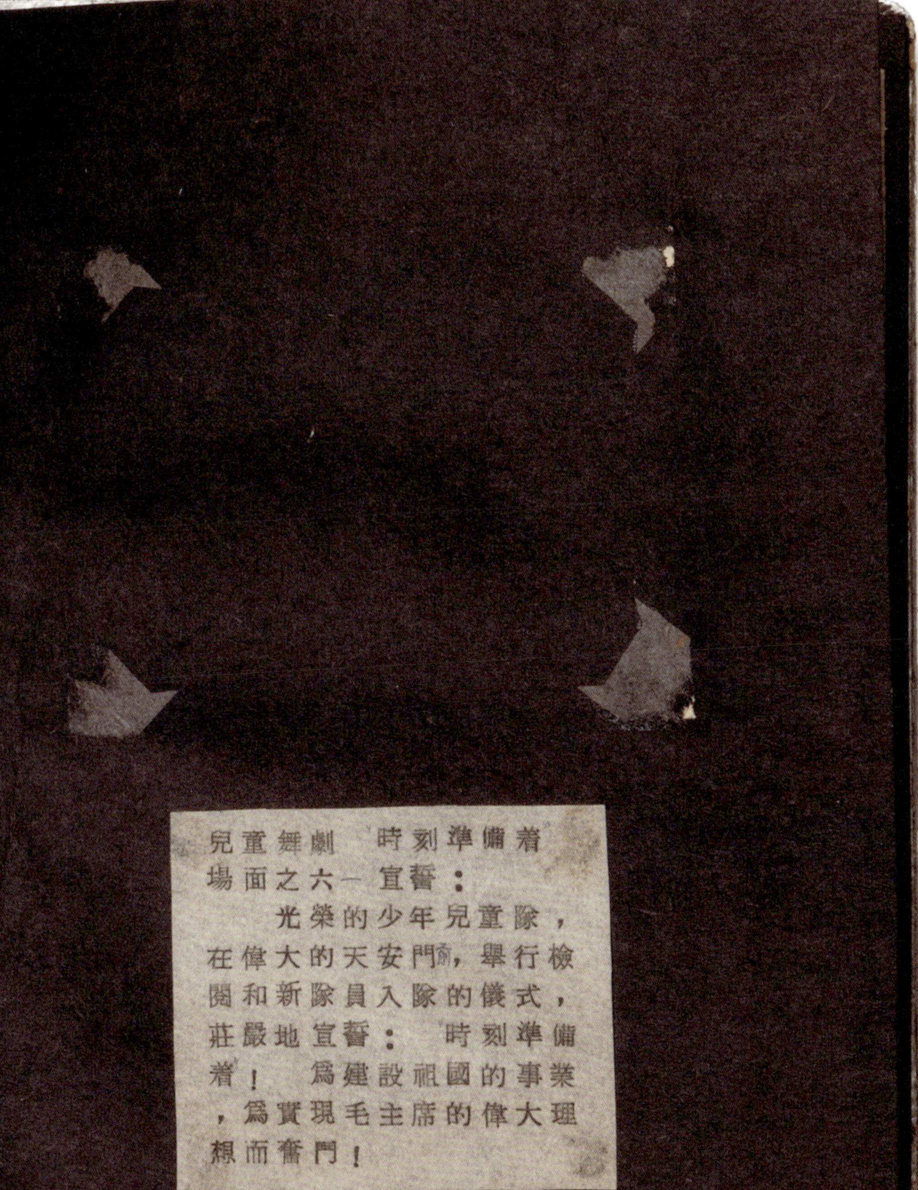

兒童舞劇　時刻準備着
場面之六一宣誓：

光榮的少年兒童隊，在偉大的天安門，舉行檢閱和新隊員入隊的儀式，莊嚴地宣誓：　時刻準備着！　爲建設祖國的事業，爲實現毛主席的偉大理想而奮鬥！

На память
дорогим Гале, Юре и
детям от нас
Феодосия, Вали.

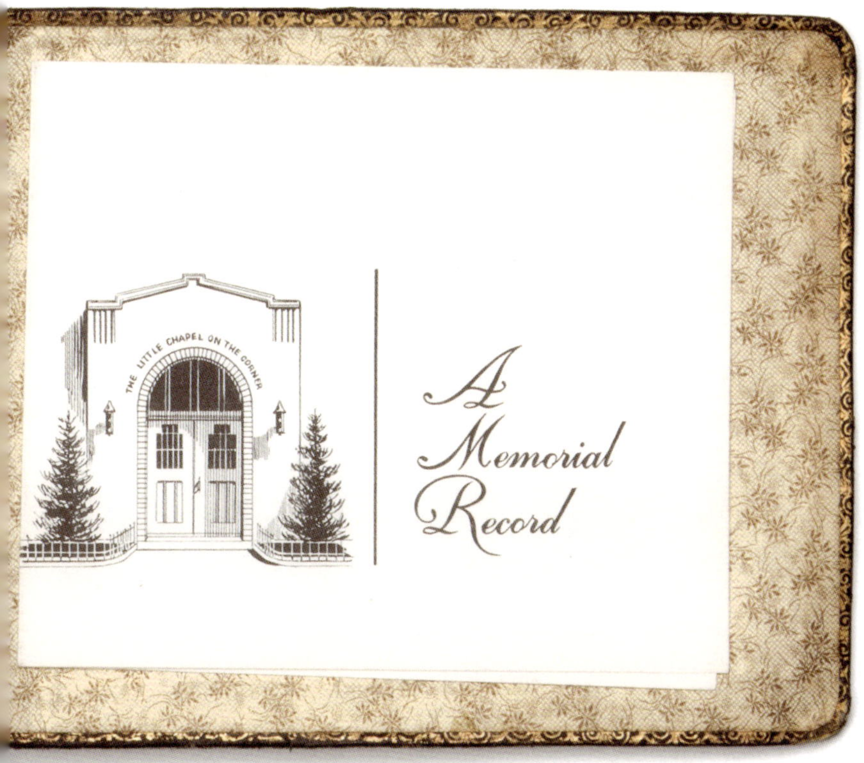
THE LITTLE CHAPEL ON THE CORNER
A Memorial Record

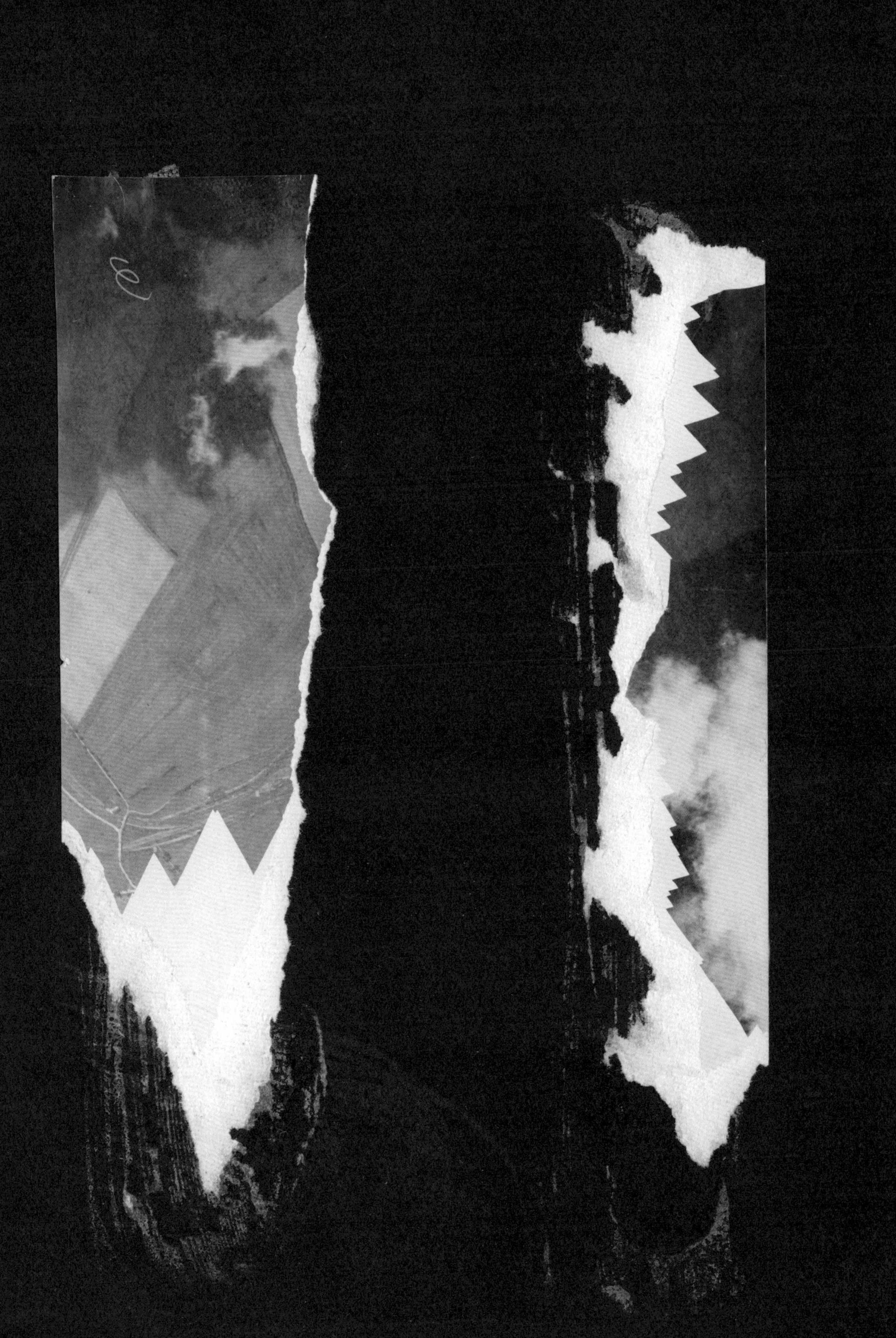

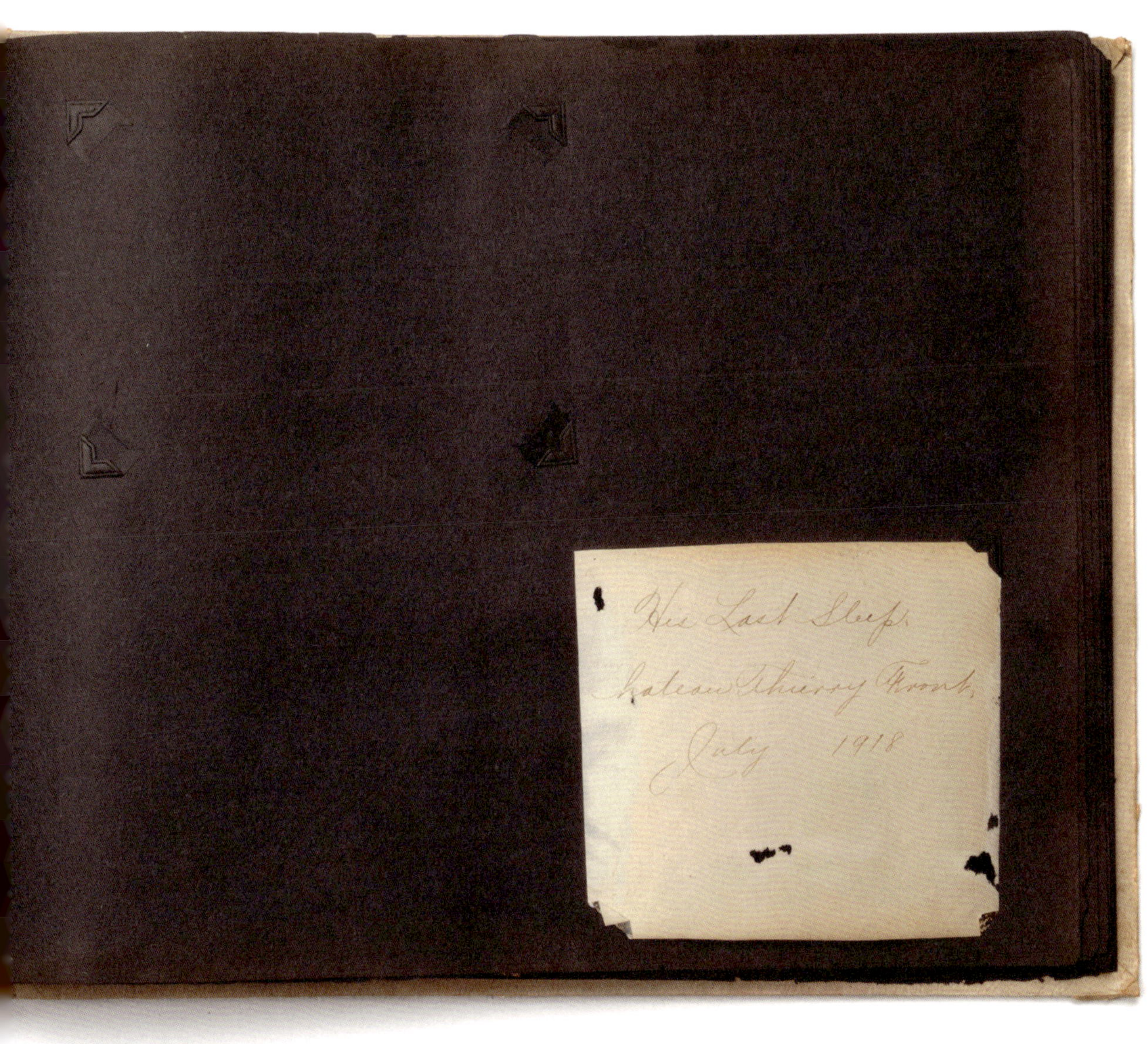
His Last Sleep.
Chateau Thierry Front.
July 1918

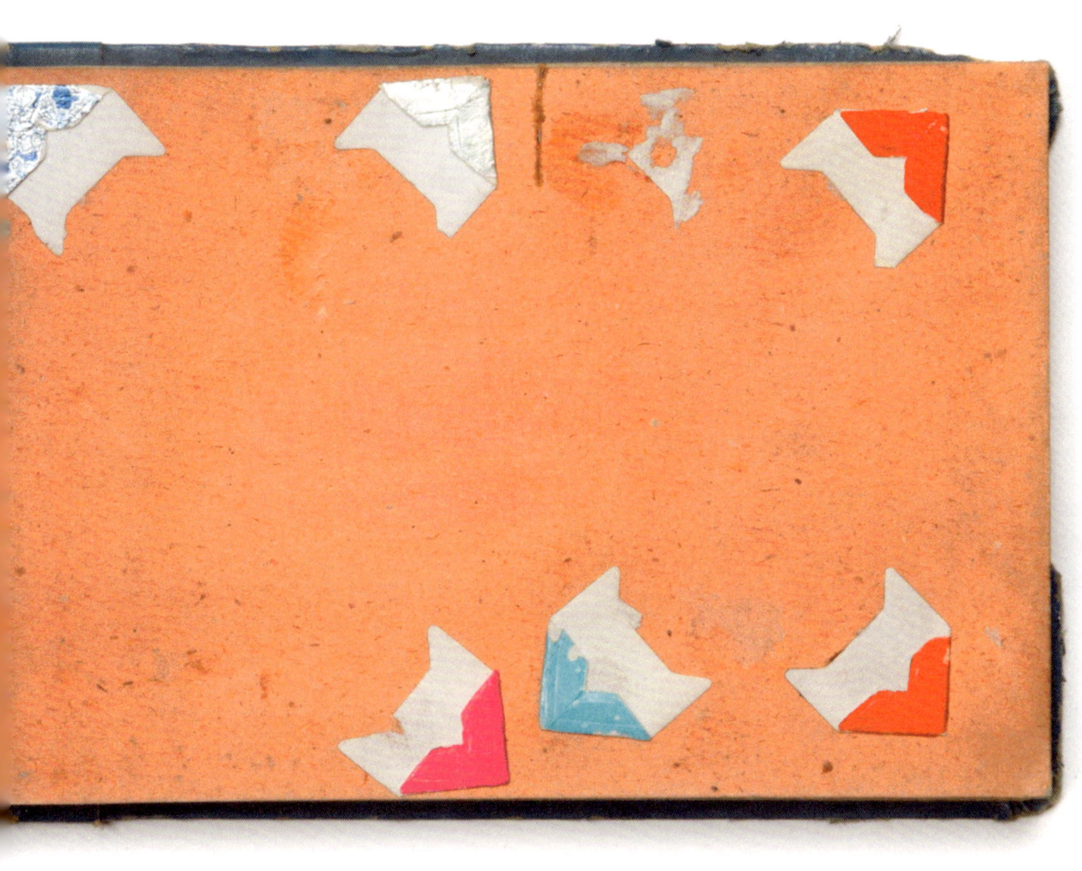

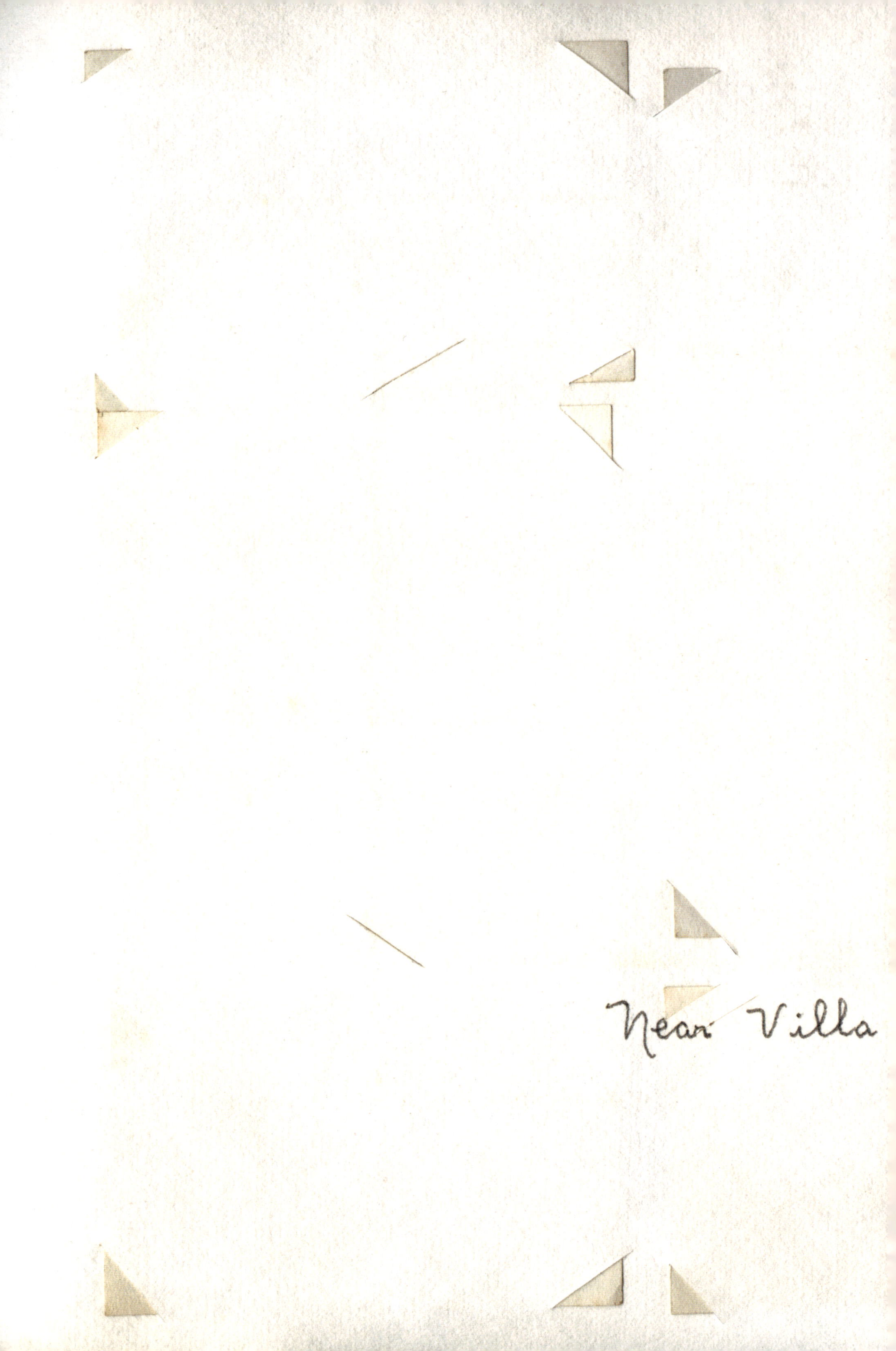
Near Villa

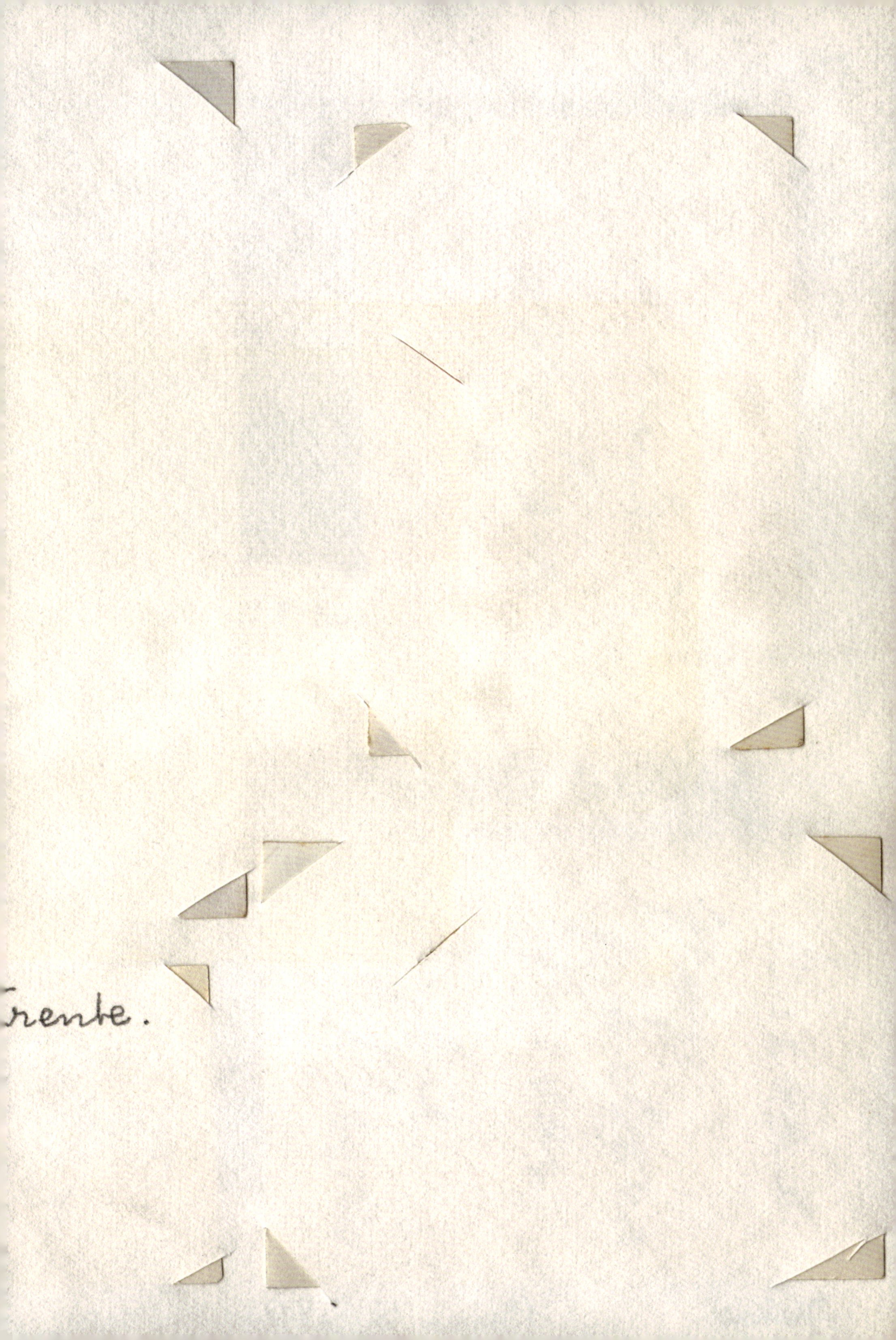
rente.

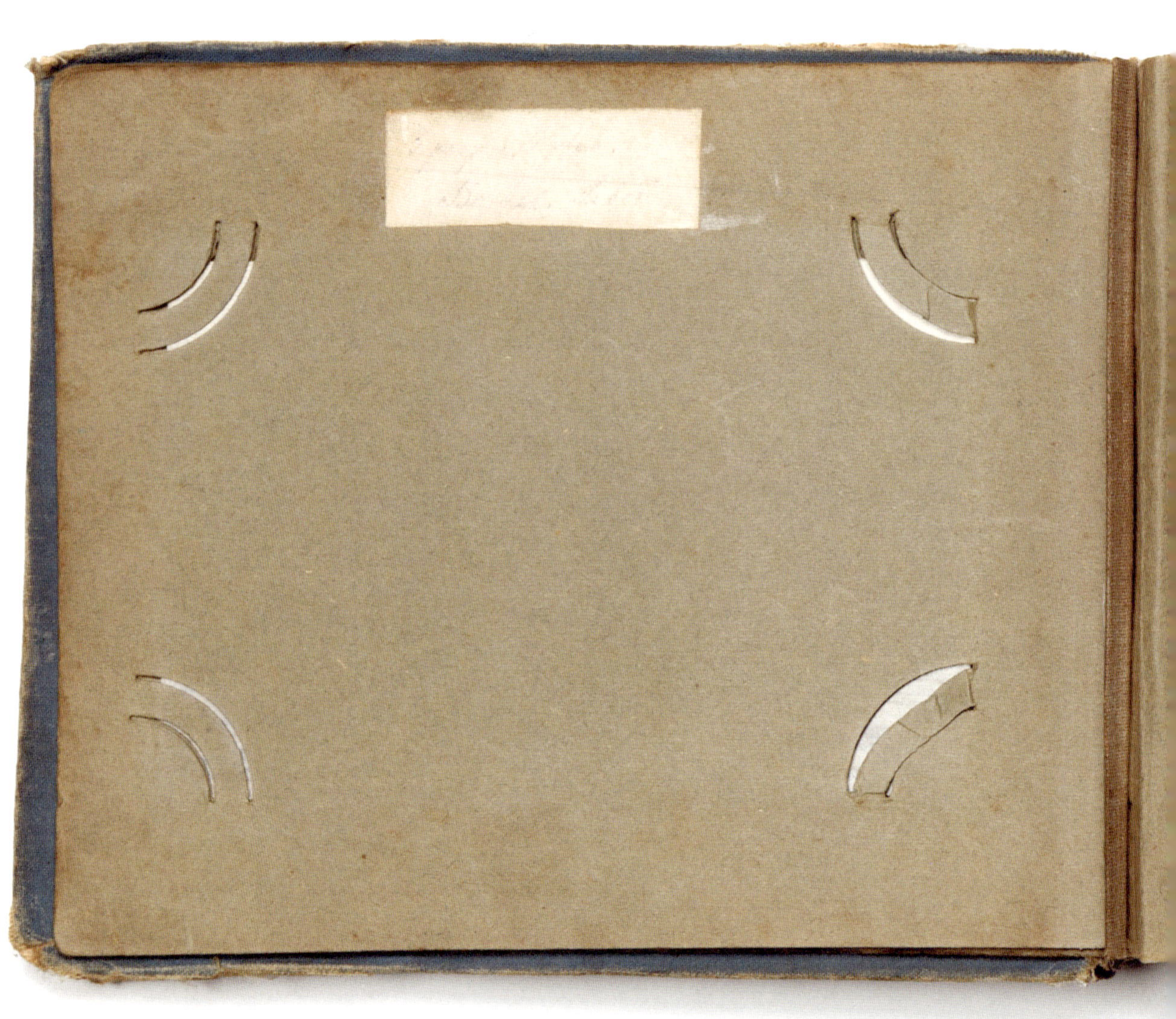

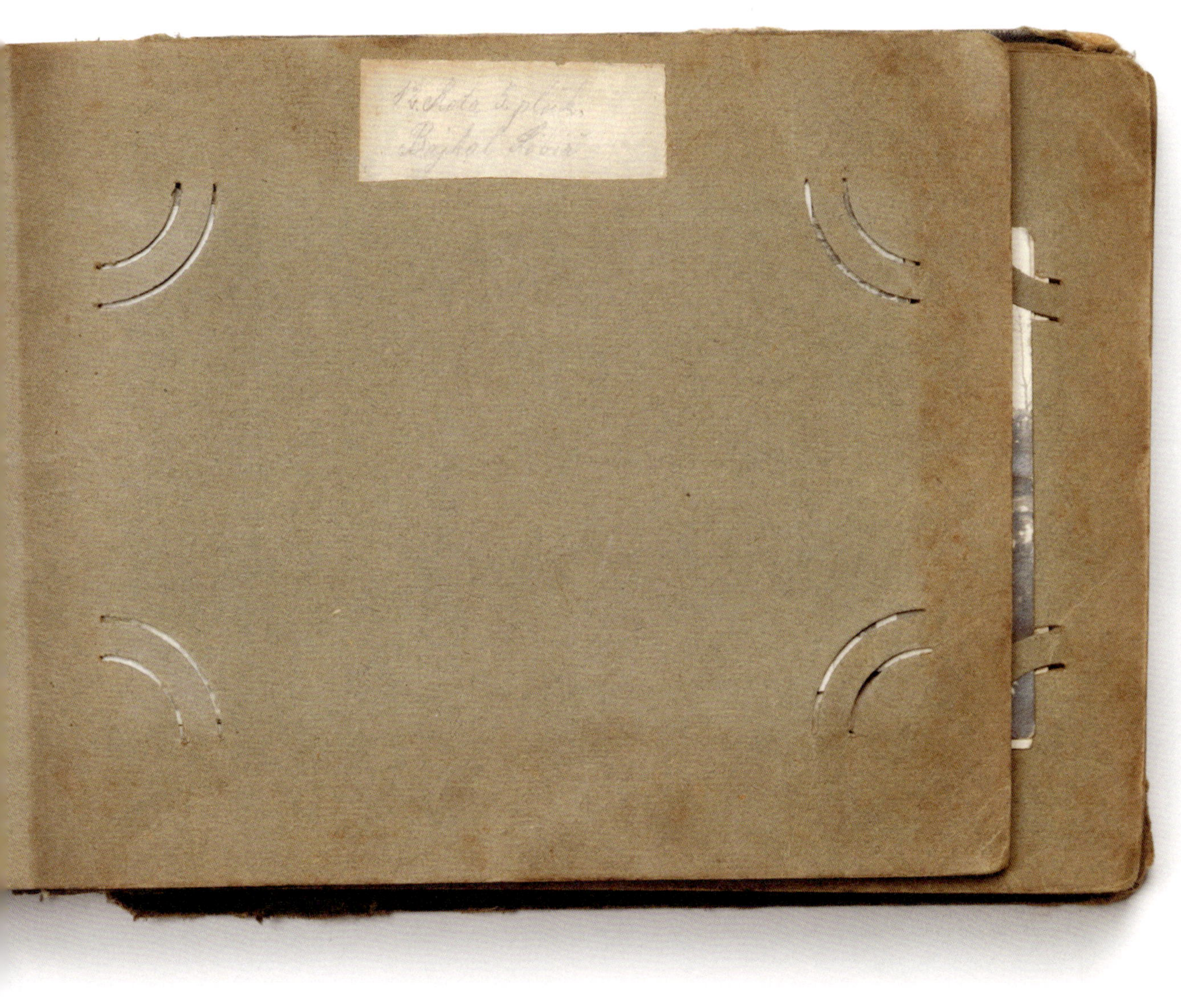

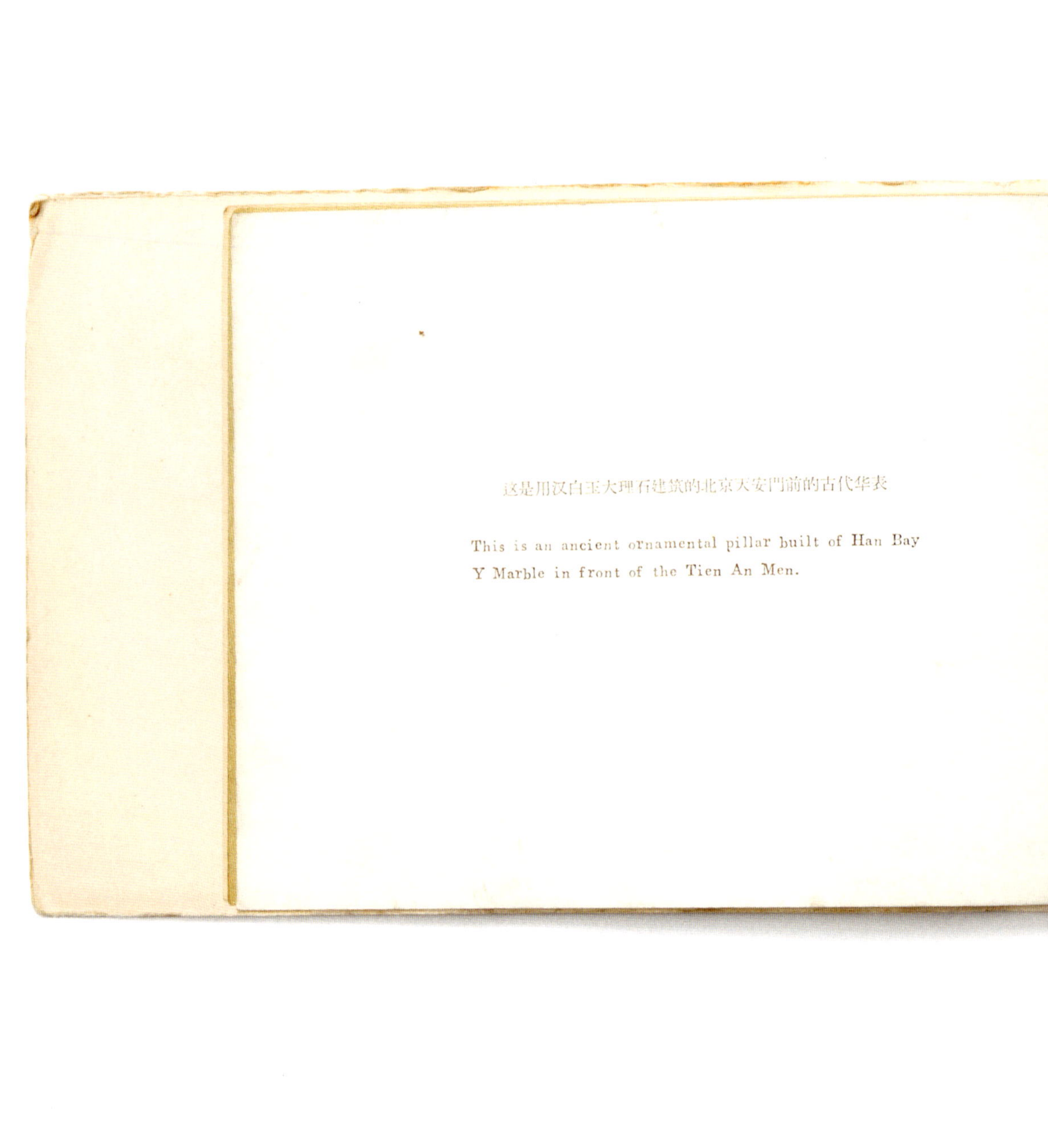

这是用汉白玉大理石建筑的北京天安門前的古代华表

This is an ancient ornamental pillar built of Han Bay Y Marble in front of the Tien An Men.

TMNo.001

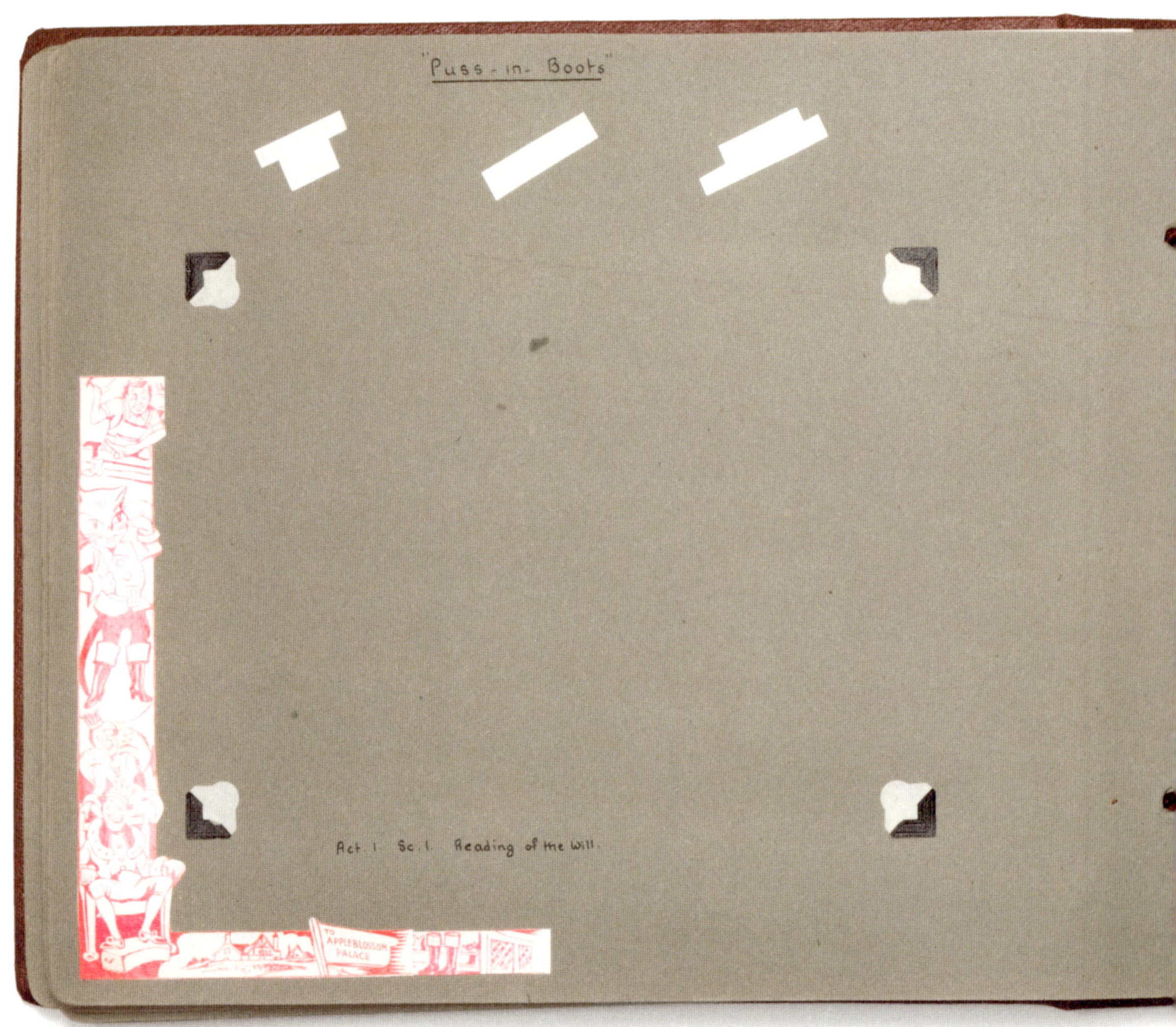
"Puss-in-Boots"
TO APPLEBLOSSOM PALACE
Act. 1. Sc. 1. Reading of the Will.

"Puss-in-Boots"

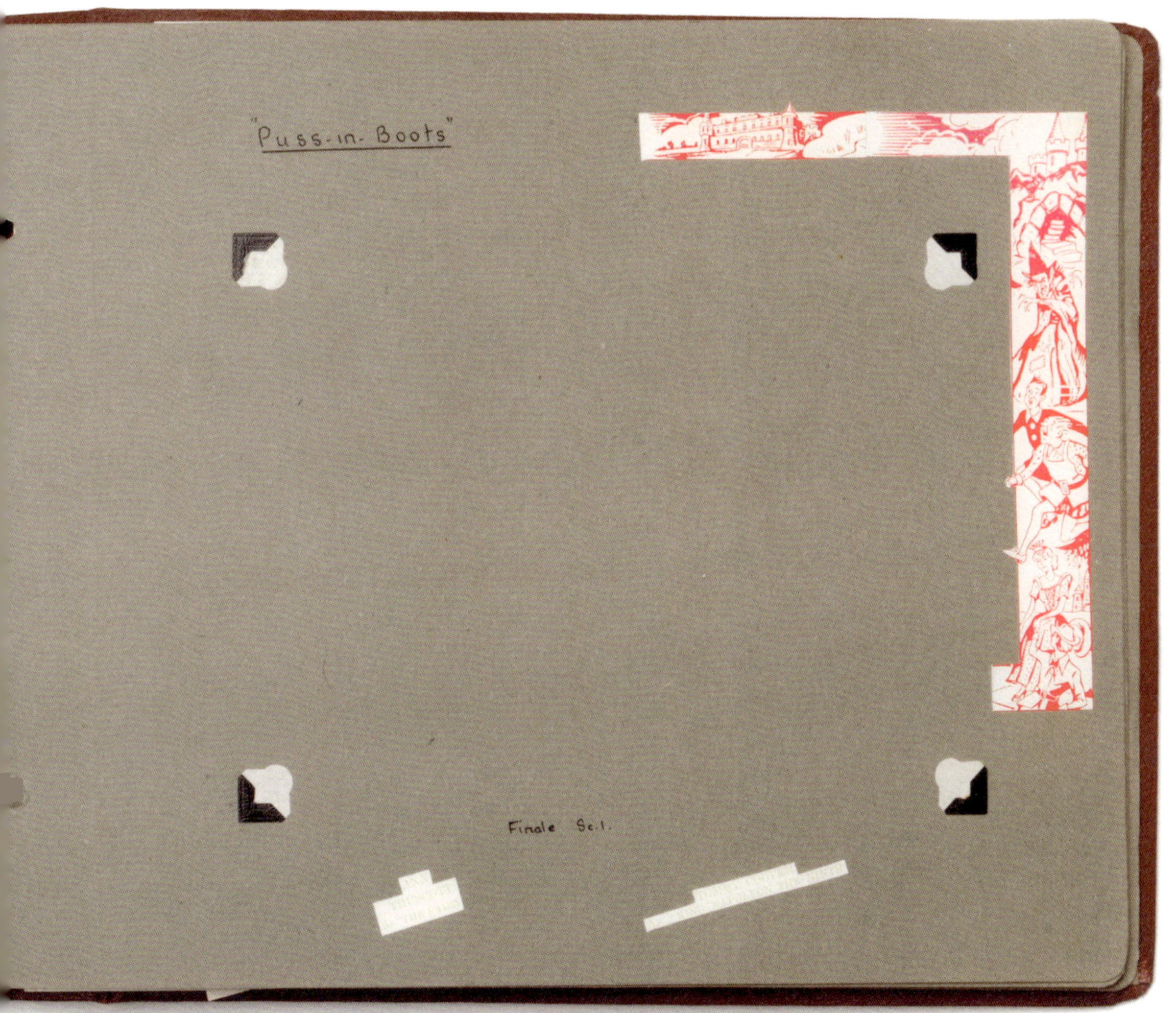

Finale Sc.1.

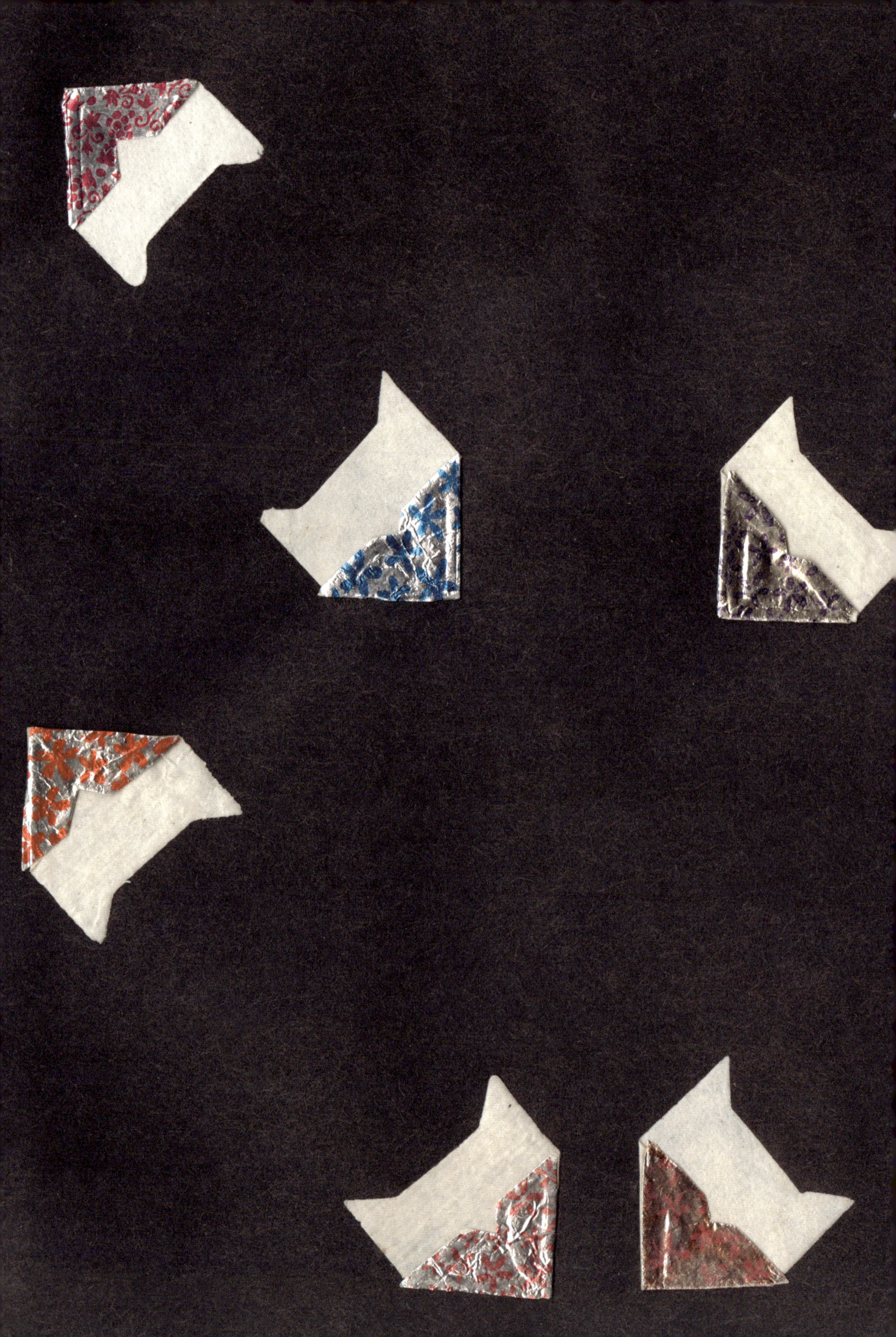

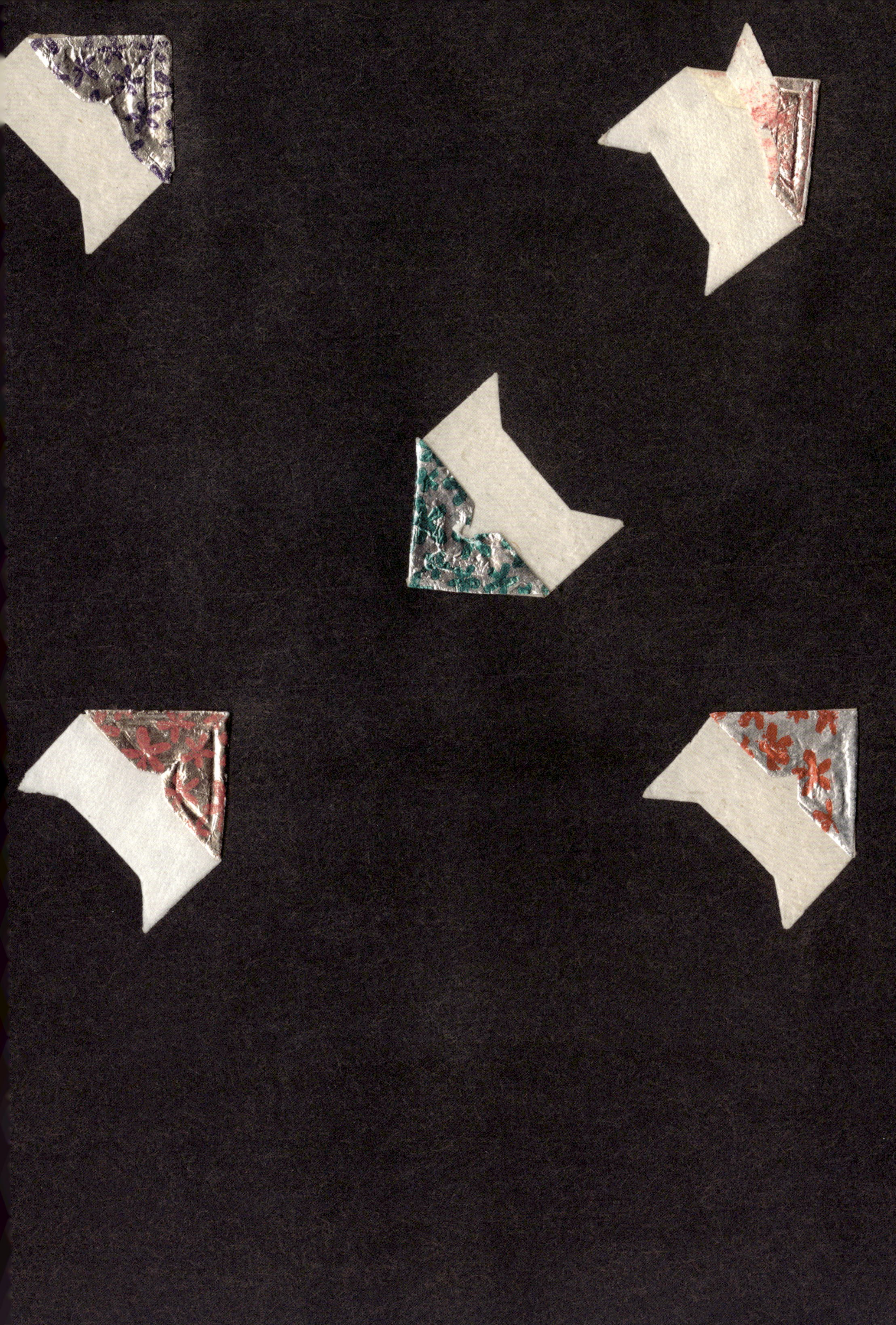

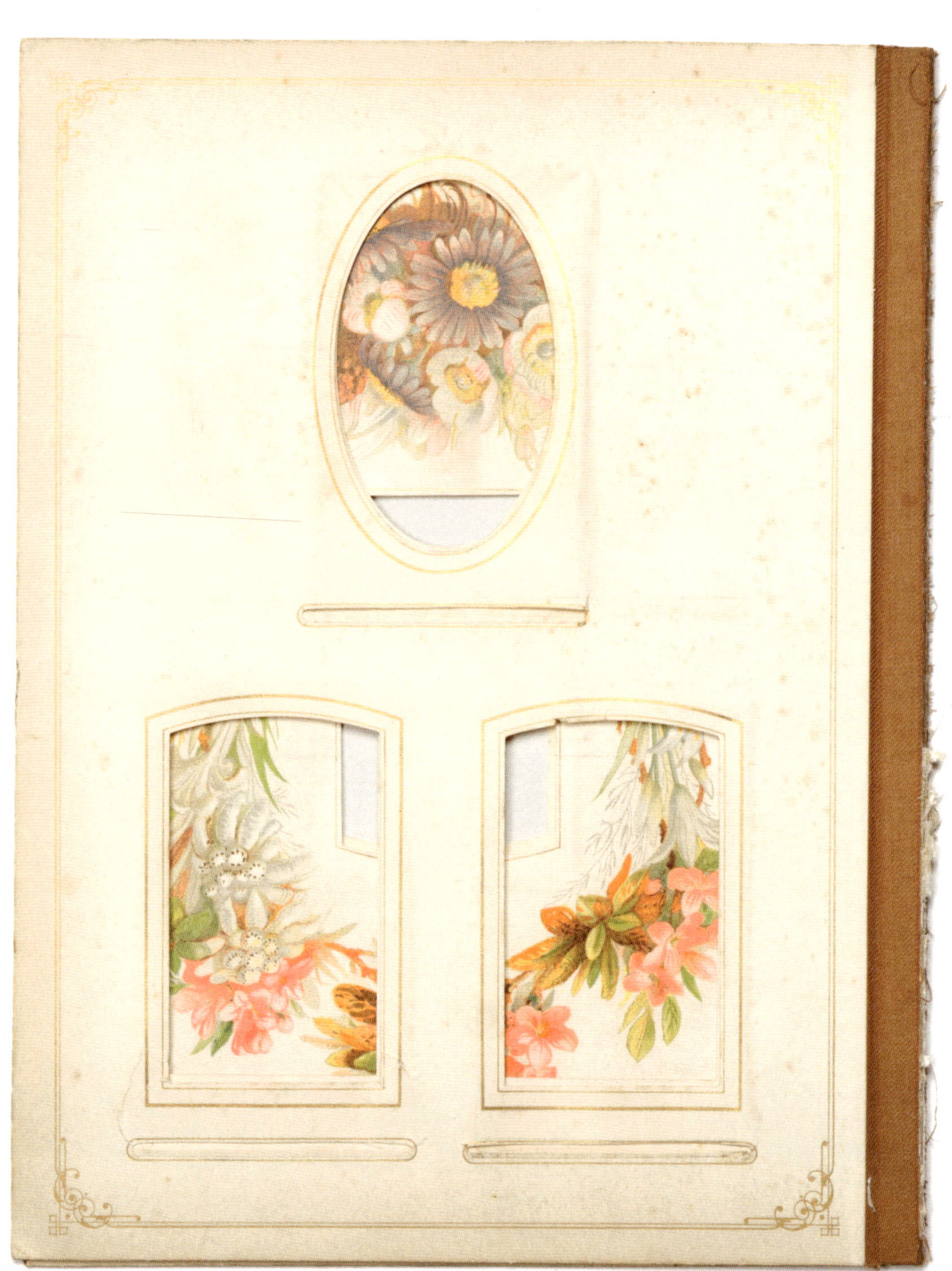

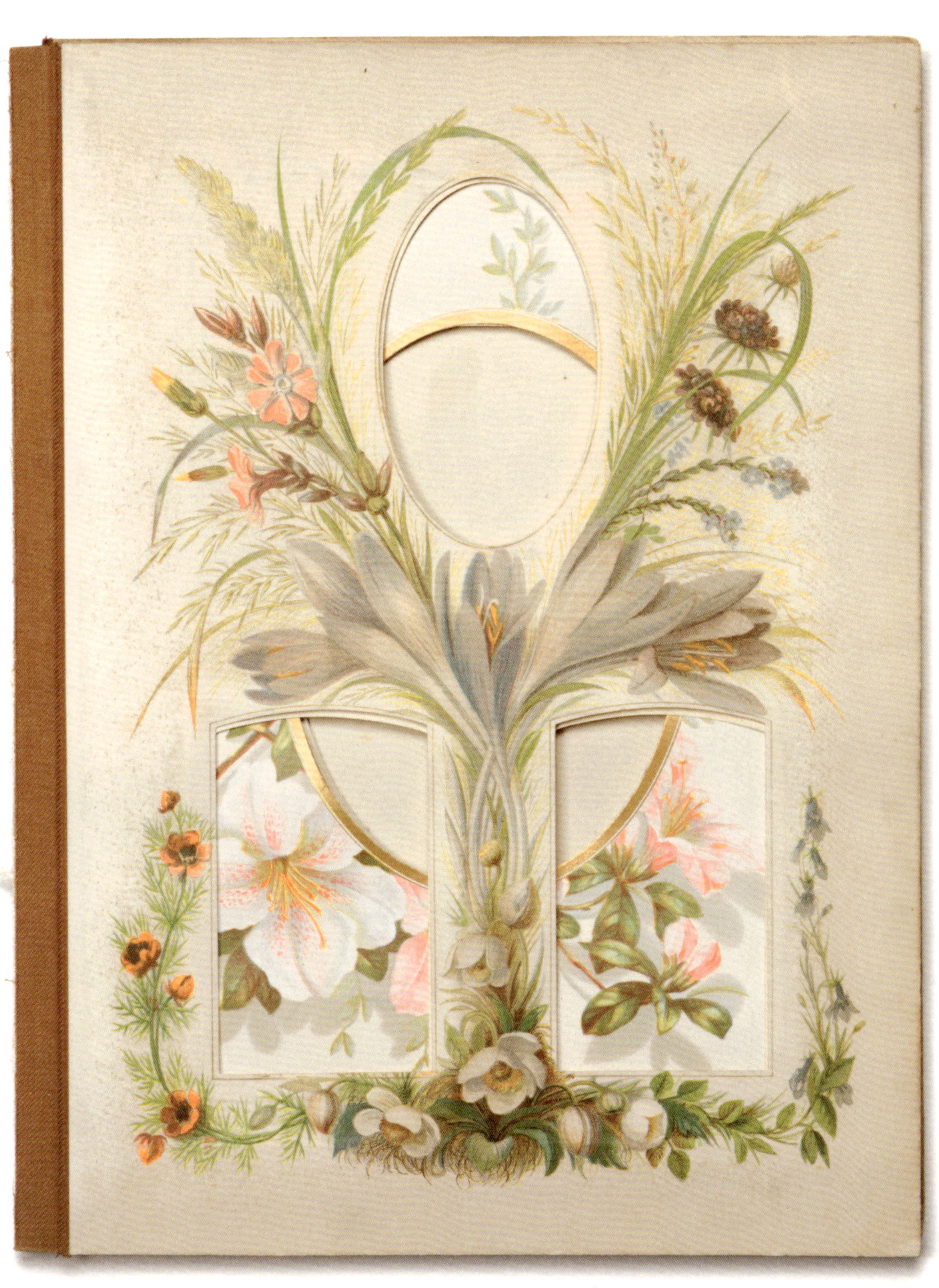

Nr. 398 165

Nr. 399 165

Nr. 400 165

Nr. 401 165

Nr. 402 ~~165~~ 164

15 20ФФВ 09г БИЛ

I WISH YOU MANY HAPP

July, 18

RETURNS OF THIS DAY

1951

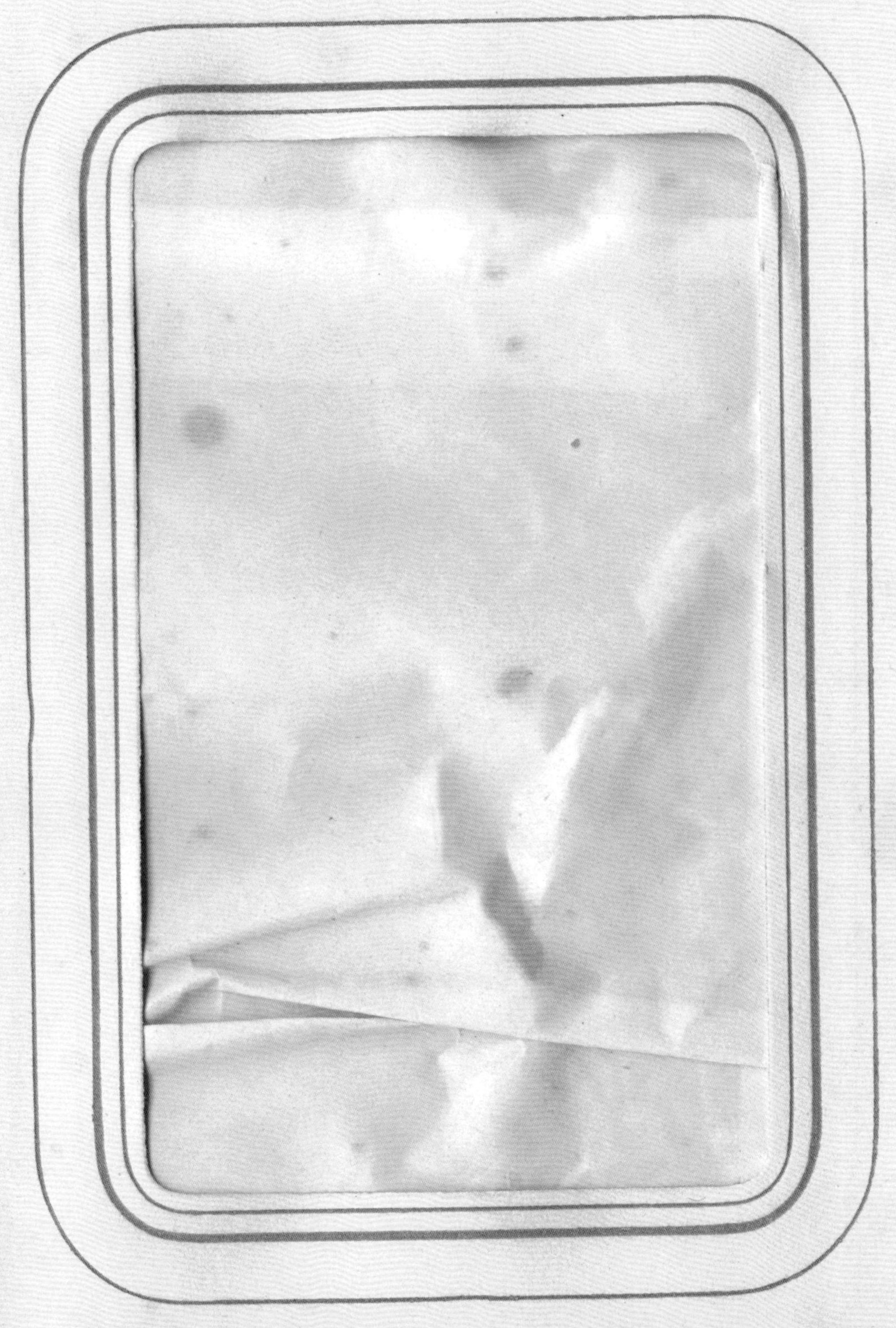

The lost picture